Routledge Library Editions

THEORY OF ECONOMIC DYNAMICS

ECONOMICS

KEYNESIAN &
POST-KEYNESIAN ECONOMICS
In 11 Volumes

THEORY OF ECONOMIC DYNAMICS

An Essay on Cyclical and Long-Run Changes in Capitalist Economy

M KALECKI

Routledge
Taylor & Francis Group

LONDON AND NEW YORK

First published in 1954

Reprinted in 2003 by
Routledge
2 Park Square, Milton Park, Abingdon, Oxon, OX14 4RN

Transferred to Digital Printing 2007

Routledge is an imprint of the Taylor & Francis Group

The publishers have made every effort to contact authors/copyright holders
of the works reprinted in *Routledge Library Editions – Economics*. This has
not been possible in every case, however, and we would welcome
correspondence from those individuals/companies we have been unable to
trace.

These reprints are taken from original copies of each book. In many cases
the condition of these originals is not perfect. The publisher has gone to
great lengths to ensure the quality of these reprints, but wishes to point
out that certain characteristics of the original copies will, of necessity, be
apparent in reprints thereof.

British Library Cataloguing in Publication Data
A CIP catalogue record for this book
is available from the British Library

Theory of Economic Dynamics
ISBN 0-415-31373-2
ISBN 0-415-31367-8

Miniset: Keynesian & Post-Keynesian Economics

Series: Routledge Library Editions – Economics

Printed and bound by CPI Antony Rowe, Eastbourne

Theory of
Economic Dynamics

An Essay on
Cyclical and Long-Run Changes
in
Capitalist Economy

by M. Kalecki

Routledge
Taylor & Francis Group

LONDON AND NEW YORK

in 11-*point Times Roman type*

Foreword

This volume is published in lieu of second editions of my *Essays in the Theory of Economic Fluctuations* and my *Studies in Economic Dynamics*. Nevertheless this is essentially a new book. Although it covers the same ground as the previous two books and the basic ideas are not much changed, the presentation and even the argument have been substantially altered. Moreover, in some instances, especially in Chapters 13 and 14, new subjects have been introduced. The scope of statistical illustrations has also been considerably widened and statistical material which has become available in the meantime has been utilized.

It may be noticed at this point that in the statistical analysis the least squares method is used. This may appear somewhat crude in the light of recent developments in statistical technique. It should be observed, however, that the purpose of the statistical analysis here is to show the plausibility of the relations between economic variables arrived at theoretically rather than to obtain the most likely coefficients of these relations. It is hoped that the precautions taken in the application of our simple statistical tools (especially in the analysis of the determinants of investment) are adequate to obtain first approximations for illustrative purposes.

Frequent use is made of formulae but an effort has been made—in some instances even at the expense of precision—to apply elementary mathematics only.

I am very much indebted to Mrs. Ting Kuan Shu-Chuang and to Mr. Chang Tse-Chun for valuable suggestions with respect to improvement of presentation and for assistance in statistical research.

M. KALECKI

February 1952

Contents

Part 1

---

*Degree of Monopoly
and Distribution of Income*

1

Cost and Prices

'Cost-determined' and 'demand-determined' prices

Short-term price changes may be classified into two broad groups: those determined mainly by changes in cost of production and those determined mainly by changes in demand. Generally speaking, changes in the prices of finished goods are 'cost-determined' while changes in the prices of raw materials inclusive of primary foodstuffs are 'demand-determined.' The prices of finished goods are affected, of course, by any 'demand-determined' changes in the prices of raw materials but it is through the channel of *costs* that this influence is transmitted.

It is clear that these two types of price formation arise out of different conditions of supply. The production of finished goods is elastic as a result of existing reserves of productive capacity. When demand increases it is met mainly by an increase in the volume of production while prices tend to remain stable. The price changes which do occur result mainly from changes in costs of production.

The situation with respect to raw materials is different. The increase in the supply of agricultural products requires a relatively considerable time. This is true, although not to the same extent, with respect to mining. With supply inelastic in short periods, an increase in demand causes a diminution of stocks and a consequent increase in price. This initial price movement may be enhanced by the addition of a speculative element. The commodities in question are normally standardized and are subject to quotation at commodity exchanges. A primary rise in demand which causes an increase in prices is frequently accompanied by secondary speculative demand. This makes it even more difficult in the short run for production to catch up with demand.

The present chapter will be devoted mainly to the study of the formation of 'cost-determined' prices.

Price fixing by a firm

Let us consider a firm with a given capital equipment. It is assumed that supply is elastic, i.e. that the firm operates below the point of practical capacity and that the prime costs (cost of materials and wages[1]) per unit of output are stable over the relevant range of output.[2] In view of the uncertainties faced in the process of price fixing it will not be assumed that the firm attempts to maximize its profits in any precise sort of manner. Nevertheless, it will be assumed that the actual level of overheads does not directly influence the determination of price since the total of overhead costs remains roughly stable as output varies. Thus, the level of output and prices at which the sum of overheads and profits may be supposed to be highest is at the same time the level which may be considered to be most favourable to profits. (It will be seen at a later stage, however, that the level of overheads may have an indirect influence upon price formation.)

In fixing the price the firm takes into consideration its average prime costs and the prices of other firms producing similar products. The firm must make sure that the price does not become too high in relation to prices of other firms, for this would drastically reduce sales, and that the price does not become too low in relation to its average prime cost, for this would drastically reduce the profit margin. Thus, when the price p is determined by the firm in relation to unit prime cost u, care is taken that the ratio of p to the weighted average price of all firms, $\bar{p}$[3], does not become too high. If u increases, p can be increased proportionately only if $\bar{p}$ rises proportionately as well. But if $\bar{p}$ increases less than u, the firm's price p will also be raised less than u. These conditions are clearly satisfied by the formula

$$p = mu + n\bar{p} \qquad (1)$$

[1] Salaries are included in overheads.
[2] In fact unit prime costs fall somewhat in many instances as output increases. We abstract from this complication which is of no major importance.
The assumption of an almost horizontal short-run prime cost curve was made in my *Essays in the Theory of Economic Fluctuations*, back in 1939. Since that time it has been proved by many empirical inquiries and has played explicitly or implicitly an important role in economic research. (Cf., for instance, W. W. Leontief: *The Structure of American Economy*, 1941, Harvard University Press.)
[3] Weighted by the respective outputs and inclusive of the firm in question.

where both m and n are positive coefficients.

We postulate that $n < 1$ and this for the following reason. In the case where the price p of the firm considered is equal to the average price $\bar{p}$ we have:

$$p = mu + np$$

from which it follows that n must be less than one.

The coefficients m and n characterizing the price-fixing policy of the firm reflect what may be called the degree of monopoly of the firm's position. Indeed, it is clear that equation (1) describes semi-monopolistic price formation. Elasticity of supply and stability of unit prime costs over the relevant range of output is incompatible with so-called perfect competition. For, if perfect competition were to prevail the excess of the price p over the unit prime costs u would drive the firm to expand its output up to the point where full capacity is reached. Thus, any firm remaining in the business would work up to capacity, and the price would be pushed up to the level which equilibrates demand and supply.

For the analysis of changes in the degree of monopoly it is convenient to use diagrammatic presentation. Let us divide equation (1) by the unit prime cost u:

$$\frac{p}{u} = m + n\frac{\bar{p}}{u}$$

This equation is represented in Fig. 1, where $\dfrac{\bar{p}}{u}$ is taken as

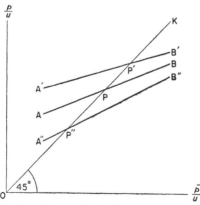

FIG. 1. Changes in the degree of monopoly.

13

abscissa and $\frac{p}{u}$ as ordinate, by a straight line AB. The inclination of AB is less than $45°$ because $n < 1$. The position of this straight line which is fully determined by m and n reflects the degree of monopoly. When, as a result of change in m and n, the straight line moves up from the position AB to that of $A'B'$, then to a given average price $\bar{p}$ and unit prime cost u there corresponds a higher price p of the firm over the relevant range of $\frac{\bar{p}}{u}$. We shall say in this case that the degree of monopoly increases. When, on the other hand, the straight line moves down to the position $A''B''$ we shall say that the degree of monopoly diminishes. (We assume that m and n always change in such a way that none of the lines corresponding to various positions of AB intersects each other over the relevant range of $\frac{\bar{p}}{u}$.)

We may now demonstrate a proposition which is of some importance to our future argument. Let us take into consideration the points of intersection P, P', P'' of the straight lines AB, $A'B'$, $A''B''$ with the line OK drawn through zero point at $45°$. It is clear that the higher the degree of monopoly the larger the abscissa of the respective point of intersection. Now this point is determined by the equations:

$$\frac{p}{u} = m + n\frac{\bar{p}}{u} \quad \text{and} \quad \frac{p}{u} = \frac{\bar{p}}{u}$$

It follows that the abscissa of the point of intersection is equal to $\frac{m}{1-n}$. Consequently a higher degree of monopoly will be reflected in the increase of $\frac{m}{1-n}$ and conversely.

In this section and the subsequent one the discussion of the influence of the degree of monopoly upon price formation is rather formal in character. The actual reasons for the changes in the degree of monopoly are examined at a later stage.

Price formation in an industry: a special case

We may commence the discussion of the determination of average price in an industry by considering a case where the coefficients m and n are the same for all firms, but where their

14

unit prime costs u differ. We have then on the basis of equation (1):

$$p_1 = mu_1 + n\bar{p}$$
$$p_2 = mu_2 + n\bar{p}$$
$$\cdots\cdots\cdots\cdots$$
$$p_k = mu_k + n\bar{p}$$

(1')

If these equations are weighted by their respective outputs (that is, each multiplied by its respective output, all added and the sum divided by the aggregate output) we obtain:

$$\bar{p} = m\bar{u} + n\bar{p}$$

so that

$$\bar{p} = \frac{m}{1-n}\bar{u}$$

(2)

Let us recall that according to the preceding section the higher the degree of monopoly the higher is $\frac{m}{1-n}$. We thus can conclude: The average price $\bar{p}$ is proportionate to the average unit prime cost $\bar{u}$ if the degree of monopoly is given. If the degree of monopoly increases, $\bar{p}$ rises in relation to $\bar{u}$.

It is still important to see in what way a new 'price equilibrium' is reached when the unit prime costs change as a result of changes in prices of raw materials or unit wage costs. Let us denote the 'new' unit prime costs by u_1, u_2, etc., and the 'old' prices by p'_1, p'_2, etc. The weighted average of these prices is $\bar{p}'$. To this correspond new prices p''_1, p''_2, etc., equal to $mu_1 + n\bar{p}'$, $mu_2 + n\bar{p}'$, etc. This leads in turn to a new average price, $\bar{p}''$, and so on, the process finally converging to a new value of $\bar{p}$ given by formula (2). This convergence of the process depends on the condition $n < 1$. Indeed, from equations (1') we have:

$$\bar{p}'' = m\bar{u} + n\bar{p}'$$

and for the new final $\bar{p}$:

$$\bar{p} = m\bar{u} + n\bar{p}$$

Subtracting the latter equation from the former we obtain:

$$\bar{p}'' - \bar{p} = n(\bar{p}' - \bar{p})$$

which shows that the deviation from the final value $\bar{p}$ diminishes in geometric progression, given $n < 1$.

15

Price formation in an industry: general case

We shall now consider the general case where the coefficients m and n differ from firm to firm. It appears that by a procedure similar to that applied in the special case the formula

$$\bar{p} = \frac{\bar{m}}{1 - \bar{n}} \bar{u} \qquad (2')$$

is reached. $\bar{m}$ and $\bar{n}$ are weighted averages of the coefficients m and n.[1]

Let us now imagine a firm for which the coefficients m and n are equal to $\bar{m}$ and $\bar{n}$ for the industry. We may call it a representative firm. We may further say that the degree of monopoly of the industry is that of the representative firm. Thus, the degree of monopoly will be determined by the position of the straight line corresponding to

$$\frac{p}{u} = \bar{m} + \bar{n}\frac{\bar{p}}{u}$$

A rise in the degree of monopoly will be reflected in the upward shift of this straight line (see Fig. 1). It follows from the argument on p. 14 that the higher the degree of monopoly, according to this definition, the higher is $\dfrac{\bar{m}}{1 - \bar{n}}$.

From this and from equation (2') there follows the generalization of the results obtained in the preceding section for a special case. The average price $\bar{p}$ is proportionate to the average unit prime cost $\bar{u}$ if the degree of monopoly is given. If the degree of monopoly increases, p rises in relation to $\bar{u}$.

The ratio of average price to average prime cost is equal to the ratio of the aggregate proceeds of industry to aggregate prime costs of industry. It follows that the ratio of proceeds to prime costs is stable, increases or diminishes depending on what happens to the degree of monopoly.

It should be recalled that all of the results obtained here are subject to the assumption of elastic supply. When firms reach their practical capacity a further rise in demand will cause a price increase beyond the level indicated by the above considerations. However, this level might be maintained for some time while the firm allows orders to pile up.

[1] $\bar{m}$ is the average of m weighted by total prime costs of each firm; $\bar{n}$ is the average of n weighted by respective outputs.

16

Causes of change in the degree of monopoly

We shall confine ourselves herein to a discussion of the major factors underlying changes in the degree of monopoly in modern capitalist economies. First and foremost the process of concentration in industry leading to the formation of giant corporations should be considered. The influence of the emergence of firms representing a substantial share of the output of an industry can be readily understood in the light of the above considerations. Such a firm knows that its price p influences appreciably the average price $\bar{p}$ and that, moreover, the other firms will be pushed in the same direction because their price formation depends on the average price $\bar{p}$. Thus, the firm can fix its price at a level higher than would otherwise be the case. The same game is played by other big firms and thus the degree of monopoly increases substantially. This state of affairs can be reinforced by tacit agreement. (Such an agreement may take inter alia the form of price fixing by one large firm, the 'leader,' while other firms follow suit.) Tacit agreement, in turn, may develop into a more or less formal cartel agreement which is equivalent to full scale monopoly restrained merely by fear of new entrants.

The second major influence is the development of sales promotion through advertising, selling agents, etc. Thus, price competition is replaced by competition in advertising campaigns, etc. These practices also will obviously cause a rise in the degree of monopoly.

In addition to the above, two other factors must be considered: (a) the influence of changes in the level of overheads in relation to prime costs upon the degree of monopoly, and (b) the significance of the power of trade unions.

If the level of overheads should rise considerably in relation to prime costs, there will necessarily follow a 'squeeze of profits' unless the ratio of proceeds to prime costs is permitted to rise. As a result, there may arise a tacit agreement among the firms of an industry to 'protect' profits, and consequently to increase prices in relation to unit prime costs. For instance, the increase in capital costs per unit of output as a result of the introduction of techniques which increase capital intensity may tend to raise the degree of monopoly in this way.

The factor of 'protection' of profits is especially apt to appear during periods of depression. The situation in such periods is as follows. Aggregate proceeds would fall in the same proportion as prime costs if the degree of monopoly remained unchanged. At the same time aggregate overheads by their very nature fall in depression less than prime costs. This provides a background for tacit agreements not to reduce prices in the same proportion as prime costs. As a result there is a tendency for the degree of monopoly to rise in the slump, a tendency which is reversed in the boom.[1]

Although the above considerations show a channel through which overheads may affect price formation, it is clear that their influence upon prices in our theory is much less clear-cut than that of prime costs. The degree of monopoly *may*, but need not necessarily, increase as a result of a rise in overheads in relation to prime costs. This and the emphasis on the influence of prices of other firms constitute the difference between the theory presented here and the so-called full cost theory.

Let us turn now to the problem of the influence of trade-union strength upon the degree of monopoly. The existence of powerful trade unions may tend to reduce profit margins for the following reasons. A high ratio of profits to wages strengthens the bargaining position of trade unions in their demands for wage increases since higher wages are then compatible with 'reasonable profits' at existing price levels. If after such increases are granted prices should be raised, this would call forth new demands for wage increases. It follows that a high ratio of profits to wages cannot be maintained without creating a tendency towards rising costs. This adverse effect upon the competitive position of a firm or an industry encourages the adoption of a policy of lower profit margins. Thus, the degree of monopoly will be kept down to some extent by the activity of trade unions, and this the more the stronger the trade unions are.

The changes in the degree of monopoly are not only of decisive importance for the distribution of income between workers and capitalists, but in some instances for the distribution of income within the capitalist class as well. Thus, the rise in the degree of monopoly caused by the growth of big corporations results in a relative shift of income to industries dominated by such corporations from other industries. In this way income is redistributed from small to big business.

---

[1] This is the basic tendency; however, in some instances the opposite process of cut-throat competition may develop in a depression.

The long-run and short-run cost-price relations

The cost-price relations arrived at above were based on short-run considerations. However, the only parameters which enter the equations in question are the coefficients m and n reflecting the degree of monopoly. These may, but need not necessarily, change in the long run. If m and n *are* constant, the long-run changes in prices will reflect only the long-run changes in unit prime costs. Technological progress will tend to reduce the unit prime cost u. But the *relations* between prices and unit prime costs can be affected by changes in equipment and technique only to the extent to which they influence the degree of monopoly.[1] The latter possibility was indicated above when it was mentioned that the degree of monopoly may be influenced by the level of overheads in relation to prime costs.

It should be noticed that the whole approach is in contradiction to generally accepted views. It is usually assumed that as a result of increasing intensity of capital, i.e. increasing amount of fixed capital per unit of output, there is of necessity a continuous increase in the ratio of price to unit prime cost. The view is apparently based on the assumption that the sum of overheads and profits varies in the long run roughly proportionately with the value of capital. Thus, the rise in capital in relation to output is translated into a higher ratio of overheads plus profits to proceeds, and the latter is equivalent to an increase in the ratio of prices to unit prime costs.

Now, it appears that profits plus overheads may show a long-run fall in relation to the value of capital and as a result the ratio of price to unit prime cost may remain constant even though capital increases in relation to output. This is illustrated by developments in the American manufacturing in the period from 1899 to 1914. (See Table 1.)

As will be seen from the table, fixed capital rose continuously in relation to production over the period considered, while the ratio of proceeds to prime costs remained roughly stable. This is explained by a fall in profits plus overheads in relation to the value of fixed capital (both in relation to its book value and in relation to its value at current prices).

There remains, of course, the possibility stated above that

[1] This, however, is qualified by the assumption underlying our cost-price equations, namely that the unit prime cost does not depend on the degree of utilization of equipment and that the limit of practical capacity is not reached. See p. 13.

Table 1. Capital Intensity and the Ratio of Proceeds to Prime Costs in Manufacturing in the United States, 1899–1914

Year	Ratio of real fixed capital to production	Ratio of overheads and profits to book value of fixed capital	Ratio of overheads and profits to value of fixed capital at current prices	Ratio of proceeds to prime costs
		1899 = 100		per cent
1899	100	100	100	133
1904	111	95	96	133
1909	125	89	84	133
1914	131	80	73	132

Source: National Bureau of Economic Research; Paul H. Douglas, The Theory of Wages; *United States Census of Manufactures. For details see Statistical Appendix, Note 1.*

the rise in overheads in relation to prime costs as a result of the increase in capital intensity may cause a rise in the degree of monopoly because of a tendency to 'protect' profits; this tendency, however, is by no means automatic and may not materialize, as is shown by the above example.

We have dealt above with certain questions which arise in connection with the application of our theory to the long-run phenomena. When this theory is applied to the analysis of price formation in the course of a business cycle, the problem arises whether our formulae hold good in the boom. Indeed, in such periods the utilization of equipment may reach the point of practical capacity and thus, under the pressure of demand, prices may exceed the level indicated by these formulae. It seems, however, that as a result of the availability of reserve capacities and the possibility of increasing the volume of equipment whenever bottlenecks occur, this phenomenon is not frequently encountered even in booms. In general, it seems to be restricted to war or post-war developments, where shortages of raw materials or equipment limit severely the supply in relation to demand. It is this type of increase in prices which is the basic reason for the inflationary developments prevailing in such periods.

Application to the long-run changes in United States manufacturing

As the ratio of price to unit prime cost is equal to the ratio of aggregate proceeds to aggregate prime costs, the changes in this ratio can be analysed empirically for various industries on the basis of the United States Census of Manufactures which gives the value of products, the cost of materials and the wage bill for each industry. However, the changes in the ratio of proceeds to prime costs for a single industry which, according to the above, is determined by changes in the degree of monopoly, reflect changes in conditions particular to that industry. For instance, a change in the price policy of one big firm may cause a fundamental change in the degree of monopoly in that industry. For this reason we limit our considerations here to the manufacturing industry as a whole, and thus are able to interpret the changes in the ratio of proceeds to prime cost in terms of major changes in industrial conditions.

We thus take into consideration the ratio of the aggregate proceeds of United States manufacturing to its aggregate prime costs. The following difficulty, however, arises. This ratio does not reflect merely the changes in the ratios of proceeds to prime costs of single industries, but also shifts in their importance in manufacturing as a whole. For this reason, in Table 2 is given not only the ratio of proceeds to prime costs of United States manufacturing, but also such a ratio calculated on the assumption that from one period to another the relative share of major industrial groups in the aggregate value of proceeds is stable.[1] The actual difference between these two series appears to be in general not significant.

Table 2. **Ratio of Proceeds to Prime Costs in Manufacturing in the United States, 1879–1937**

Year	Original data	Assuming stable industrial composition, base year 1899
		(in percentages)
1879	122·5	124·0
1889	131·7	131·0
1899	133·3	133·3
1914	131·6	131·4
1923	133·0	132·7
1929	139·4	139·6
1937	136·3	136·8

Source: *United States Census of Manufactures.*

[1] The details of the calculation, as well as the adjustments which have been made in order to assure approximate comparability for various census years which was upset by the changes in the scope and methods of the Census, are described in the Statistical Appendix, Notes 2 and 3.

It will be seen that there is a substantial increase in the ratio of proceeds to prime costs from 1879 to 1889. It is generally known that this period marked a change in American capitalism characterized by the formation of giant industrial corporations. It is thus not surprising that the degree of monopoly increased in that period.

From 1889 to 1923 there is little change in the ratio of proceeds to prime costs. A marked increase, however, appears again in the period 1923–1929. The rise in the degree of monopoly in this period is partly accounted for by what may be called a 'commercial revolution'—a rapid introduction of sales promotion through advertising, selling agents, etc. Another factor was a general increase in overheads in relation to prime costs which occurred in this period.

It may be questioned whether the high level of the ratio of proceeds to prime costs in 1929 was not due, at least partly, to firms reaching their full capacity in the boom. It should be noticed, however, that the degree of utilization of equipment was not higher in 1929 than in 1923. It also appears from the consideration of the Census figures in 1925 and 1927 that the rise in ratio of proceeds to prime costs in the period 1923–1929 was gradual in character.

From 1929 to 1937 the ratio of proceeds to prime costs shows a moderate reduction. This can probably be attributed largely to the rise in the power of trade unions.

The explanations given here are tentative and sketchy in character. Indeed, the interpretation of the movement of the ratio of proceeds to prime cost in terms of changes in the degree of monopoly is really the task of the economic historian who can contribute to such a study a more thorough knowledge of changing industrial conditions.

Application to United States manufacturing and retail trade during the Great Depression

In Table 3 the ratio of proceeds to prime costs for United States manufacturing is given for 1929, 1931, 1933, 1935 and 1937. Again, in addition to the original ratio of proceeds to prime cost the ratio adjusted for changes in composition in the value of products is given.[1] As in the previous table, the

1 As in the preceding table, the figures were adjusted for changes in the scope and methods of the Census (see Statistical Appendix, Notes 2 and 3).

two series do not differ significantly. For this period the ratio of aggregate retail sales of consumption goods in the United States to their cost to retailers is also available. This corresponds roughly to the ratio of proceeds to prime costs for the retail trade and is included in Table 3 (a series adjusted for composition of sales was not calculated).

Table 3. Ratio of Proceeds to Prime Costs in Manufacturing and Retail Trade in the United States, 1929–1937

Year	Ratio of proceeds to prime costs in manufacturing industries		Ratio of sales to costs in retail trade
	Original data	Assuming stable industrial composition, base year 1929	
		(in percentages)	
1929	139·4	139·4	142·0
1931	143·3	142·2	144·7
1933	142·8	142·3	148·8
1935	136·6	136·7	140·8
1937	136·3	136·6	140·7

Source: United States Census of Manufactures; B. M. Fowler and W. H. Shaw, 'Distributive Costs of Consumption Goods,' Survey of Current Business, July 1942.

It will be seen that the ratio of proceeds to prime costs tended to increase in the depression; but taking into consideration the extent of the depression in the 'thirties the change is very moderate. The increase in the ratio can be attributed to a rise in overheads in relation to prime costs, which fostered tacit agreements to 'protect' profits and thus to raise the degree of monopoly. It will be seen that during the recovery from 1933 to 1937 there was a reverse movement. For manufacturing, however, the ratio of proceeds to prime cost fell to a level which was significantly lower than in 1929. As suggested in the preceding section, this is probably the result of a considerable strengthening of trade unions in the period 1933–1937.

Fluctuations in prices of raw materials

As stated at the beginning of this chapter, short-run changes in the prices of primary products largely reflect changes in demand. Thus they fall considerably during downswings and rise substantially during upswings.

It is known that prices of raw materials undergo larger cyclical fluctuations than wage rates. The causes of this phenomenon can be explained as follows. Even with constant wage rates the prices of raw materials would fall in a depression as a result of a slump in 'real' demand. Now, the cuts in money wages during a depression can never 'catch up' with the price of raw materials because wage cuts in turn cause a fall in demand and hence a new fall in the prices of primary products. Imagine that the prices of raw materials fall by 20 per cent as a result of the slump in real demand. Imagine further that the wage rate is cut subsequently by 20 per cent also. The theory of price formation developed above shows that the general price level will in consequence also fall by around 20 per cent. (The degree of monopoly is likely to increase somewhat but not much.) But this will cause a corresponding fall in incomes, demand, and thus in prices of raw materials.

In Table 4 below, indices of prices of raw materials and hourly earnings in the United States in the period 1929–1941 are compared.

Table 4. Indices of Prices of Raw Materials and of Hourly Earnings in Manufacturing, Mining, Construction and Railroads in the United States, 1929–1941

Year	Prices of raw materials	Hourly earnings	Ratio of prices of raw materials to hourly earnings
1929	100·0	100·0	100·0
1930	86·5	99·1	87·3
1931	67·3	94·5	71·2
1932	56·5	82·1	68·8
1933	57·9	80·9	71·6
1934	70·4	93·8	75·1
1935	79·1	98·0	80·7
1936	81·9	99·5	82·3
1937	87·0	109·6	79·4
1938	73·8	111·1	66·4
1939	72·0	112·3	64·1
1940	73·7	115·7	63·7
1941	85·6	126·6	67·6

Source: *Department of Commerce*, Statistical Abstract of the United States, Survey of Current Business, Supplement.

The ratio of prices of raw materials to hourly wages shows a long-run downward trend which in part reflects the rise in productivity of labour. This, however, does not obscure the cyclical pattern which is manifested in particular in the decided fall in both the slump of 1929–1933 and that of 1937–1938.

Price formation of finished goods

The formation of prices of finished goods according to the above theory is the result of price formation at each stage of production on the basis of the formula:

$$\bar{p} = \frac{\bar{m}}{1 - \bar{n}} \bar{u} \qquad (2')$$

With a given degree of monopoly, prices at each stage are proportionate to unit prime costs. In the first stage of production, prime costs consist of wages and the cost of primary products. In the next stage the prices are formed on the basis of the prices of the previous stage and the wages of the present stage, and so on. It is easy to see, therefore, that, with a given degree of monopoly, prices of finished goods are homogeneous linear functions of prices of primary materials on the one hand, and of wage costs at all stages of production on the other.

Since fluctuations of wages in the course of the business cycle are much smaller than those of prices of raw materials (see the preceding section) it follows directly that prices of finished goods also tend to fluctuate considerably less than prices of raw materials.

As to different categories of prices of finished goods, it has been frequently assumed that the prices of investment goods during a depression fall more than prices of consumption goods. There is no basis for such a contention in the present theory. There may even be a certain presumption in favour of some fall in the prices of consumption goods in relation to the prices of investment goods. The weight of primary products inclusive of food is probably higher in the aggregate in the case of consumption goods than in the case of investment goods and the prices of primary products fall during a depression more than wages.

In Table 5 are given the indices of prices of raw materials, of consumer prices (at retail level) and of prices of finished investment goods for the United States in the period 1929–1941. It will be seen that the prices of raw materials showed much larger fluctuations than the prices of finished consumption or investment goods.

Table 5. Indices of Prices of Raw Materials, Consumption Goods and Investment Goods in the United States, 1929–1941

Year	Prices of raw materials	Prices of consumption goods[1]	Prices of investment goods[1]	Ratio of prices of investment goods to prices of consumption goods
1929	100·0	100·0	100·0	100·0
1930	86·5	95·3	97·2	102·0
1931	67·3	85·3	89·2	104·3
1932	56·5	75·0	80·3	107·1
1933	57·9	71·5	78·3	109·5
1934	70·4	75·8	85·8	113·2
1935	79·1	77·8	84·7	108·9
1936	81·9	78·5	87·3	111·2
1937	87·0	81·5	92·4	113·4
1938	73·8	79·6	95·8	120·4
1939	72·0	78·9	94·4	119·6
1940	73·7	79·8	96·9	121·4
1941	85·6	84·8	102·9	121·3

Source: Department of Commerce, Survey of Current Business.

The ratio of the prices of investment goods to the prices of consumption goods shows a distinct rising trend. However, from the time-curve of this ratio in Fig. 2 it is apparent that

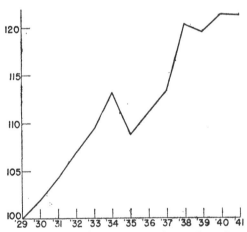

Fig. 2.   Ratio of prices of investment goods to prices of consumption goods, United States, 1929–1941.

[1] Price indices implicit in the deflation of consumption and fixed capital investment calculated from *National Income Supplement to Survey of Current Business,* 1951. It is clear that these indices are of Paasche type.

26

there was a more pronounced rise during the downswings of 1929–1933 and 1937–1938[1] than in the period considered as a whole. It appears on the other hand that these cyclical fluctuations of the ratio of the prices of investment goods to the prices of consumption goods although clearly marked are rather small in amplitude.

[1] In the latter case, however, the phenomenon seems to have been exaggerated by special factors.

2

Distribution
of National Income

Determinants of the relative share of wages in income

We shall now link the ratio of proceeds to prime costs in an industry, which we discussed in the previous chapter, with the relative share of wages in the value added of that industry. The value added, i.e. the value of products less the cost of materials, is equal to the sum of wages, overheads and profits. If we denote aggregate wages by W, the aggregate cost of materials by M, and the ratio of aggregate proceeds to aggregate prime cost by k, we have:

$$\text{overheads} + \text{profits} = (k - 1)(W + M)$$

where the ratio of proceeds to prime costs k is determined, according to the above, by the degree of monopoly. The relative share of wages in the value added of an industry may be represented as

$$w = \frac{W}{W + (k - 1)(W + M)}$$

If we denote the ratio of the aggregate cost of materials to the wage bill by j, we have:

$$w = \frac{1}{1 + (k - 1)(j + 1)} \tag{3}$$

It follows that the relative share of wages in the value added is determined by the degree of monopoly and by the ratio of the materials bill to the wage bill.

A similar formula to that established for a single industry can now be written for the manufacturing industry as a whole.

However, here the ratio of proceeds to prime costs and the ratio of the cost of materials to wages depend also on the importance of particular industries in manufacturing taken as a whole. In order to separate this element we can proceed as follows. In formula (3), for k, the ratio of proceeds to prime costs, and for j, the ratio of the materials bill to the wage bill, we substitute the ratios k' and j', adjusted in such a way as to eliminate the effect of changes in the importance of particular industries. Thus we obtain:

$$w' = \frac{1}{1 + (k' - 1)(j' + 1)} \tag{3'}$$

The relative share of wages in the value added, w', obtained in this way will deviate from the actual relative share of wages, w, by an amount which will be due to changes in the industrial composition of value added.

Of the parameters in formula (3') k' is determined by the degree of monopoly in manufacturing industries. The problem of determinants of j' is somewhat more complicated. Prices of materials are determined by the prices of primary products, by wage costs at the lower stages of production and by the degree of monopoly at those stages. Thus, roughly speaking, j', which equals the ratio of unit costs of materials to unit wage costs, is determined by the ratio of prices of primary products to unit wage costs and by the degree of monopoly in manufacturing.[1] To summarize: the relative share of wages in the value added of manufacturing is determined, apart from the industrial composition of the value added, by the degree of monopoly and by the ratio of raw material prices to unit wage costs. A rise in the degree of monopoly or in raw material prices in relation to unit wage costs causes a fall of the relative share of wages in the value added.

It should be recalled in this connection that as distinguished from prices of finished goods the prices of raw materials are 'demand determined.' The ratio of raw material prices to unit wage costs depends on the demand for raw materials, as determined by the level of economic activity, in relation to their supply which is inelastic in the short run (cf. p. 11 and p. 24).

[1] This rough generalization is based on two simplifying assumptions: (a) that unit costs of materials change proportionately with prices of materials, i.e. changing efficiency in the utilization of materials is not taken into account; and (b) that unit wage costs at the lower stages of production vary proportionately with unit wage costs at higher stages.

We can now consider in much the same way as above a group of industries broader than manufacturing where the pattern of price formation may be assumed to be similar, namely manufacturing, construction, transportation and services. For this group as a whole the relative share of wages in the aggregate value added will decrease with an increase in the degree of monopoly or an increase in the ratio of prices of primary products to unit wage costs. The result will also be affected, of course, by changes in the industrial composition of the value added of the group.

It may now be shown that this theorem can be generalized to cover the relative share of wages in the gross national income of the private sector (i.e. national income gross of depreciation exclusive of income of government employees). In addition to the sectors of the economy accounted for above, we have still to consider agriculture and mining, communications and public utilities, trade, real estate and finance. In agriculture and mining the products are raw materials and the relative share of wages in the value added depends mainly on the ratio of prices of the raw materials *produced* to their unit wage costs. In the remaining sectors the relative share of wages in the value added is negligible. It will thus be seen that, broadly speaking, the degree of monopoly, the ratio of prices of raw materials to unit wage costs and industrial composition[1] are the determinants of the relative share of wages in the gross income of the private sector.

Long-run and short-run changes in the distribution of income

The long-run changes in the relative share of wages, whether in the value added of an industrial group such as manufacturing or in the gross income of all the private sector, are, according to the above, determined by long-run trends in the degree of monopoly, in the prices of raw materials in relation to unit wage costs, and in industrial composition. The degree of monopoly has a general tendency to increase in the long run and thus to depress the relative share of wages in income, although, as we have seen above, this tendency is much stronger in some periods than in others. It is difficult, however, to generalize about the relation of raw material prices to unit wage costs (which depends

[1] It should be noticed that by industrial composition we mean the composition of the *value* of the gross income of the private sector. Thus, changes in the composition depend not only on changes in the *volume* of the industrial components but also on the relative movement of the respective prices.

on long-run changes in the demand-supply position of raw materials) or about industrial composition. No *a priori* statement is therefore possible as to the long-run trend of the relative share of wages in income. As we shall see in the next section, the relative share of wages in the value added of United States manufacturing declined considerably after 1880, whereas in the United Kingdom wages maintained their share in the national income from the 'eighties to 1924, showing long-run ups and downs in the intervening period.

It is possible to say something more specific about changes in the relative share of wages in income in the course of the business cycle. We have found that the degree of monopoly is likely to increase somewhat during depressions (cf. p. 18). Prices of raw materials fall in the slump in relation to wages (cf. p. 24). The former influence tends to reduce the relative share of wages in income and the latter to increase it. Finally, changes in industrial composition during a depression affect the relative share of wages adversely. Indeed, these changes are dominated by a reduction of investment in relation to other activities and the relative share of wages in the income of investment goods industries is generally higher than in other industries. (In communications, public utilities, trade, real estate and finance, particularly, wage payments are relatively unimportant.)

The net effect of changes in these three factors upon the relative share of wages in income—of which the first and the third are negative and the second positive—appears to be small. Thus, the relative share of wages, whether in the value added of an industrial group or in the gross income of the private sector as a whole, does not seem to show marked cyclical fluctuations.

The above may be illustrated: (*a*) by an analysis of the long-run changes in the relative share of wages in the value added of United States manufacturing and in the national income of the United Kingdom; (*b*) by an analysis of changes in the relative share of wages in the value added of United States manufacturing during the Great Depression; and (*c*) by an analysis of changes during the same period in the relative share of wages in the national income of the United States and the United Kingdom.

Long-run changes in the relative share of wages in the value added of United States manufacturing and in the national income of the United Kingdom

The long-run changes in the relative share of wages in the value added of United States manufacturing are analysed in Table 6. In the first two columns k' and j' are given, i.e. the

Table 6. Relative Share of Wages in Value Added in Manufacturing in the United States, 1879–1937

Year	Ratio of proceeds to prime costs	Ratio of materials bill to wage bill	Share of wages in value added	Share of wages in value added
	Assuming stable industrial composition (base year 1899)			Original data
	k'	j'	w'	w
		(in percentages)		
1879	124·0	355	47·8	47·8
1889	131·0	297	44·8	44·6
1899	133·3	337	40·7	40·7
1914	131·4	341	41·9	40·2
1923	132·7	292	43·8	41·3
1929	139·6	311	38·1	36·2
1937	136·3	298	40·9	38·6

Source: United States Census of Manufactures.

'adjusted' ratio of proceeds to prime costs and the 'adjusted' ratio of the materials bill to the wage bill.[1] From these two series w', the adjusted relative share of wages in the value added, is derived by employing formula (3'). Finally, the actual relative share of wages in the value added is given. The changes in the difference $w-w'$ indicate the influence of changes in the industrial composition of value added.

It appears that w, the actual relative share of wages in the value added, suffered a considerable though not quite continuous fall over the period considered. This fall resulted mainly from the increase in the 'adjusted' ratio of proceeds to prime costs, k', which in our interpretation reflects a rise in the degree of monopoly. The 'adjusted' ratio of the materials bill to the wage bill, j', tended to fall rather than to rise and thus in general its changes mitigated the decline in w. Finally, the effect of changes in industrial composition was to reduce the actual relative share

[1] The 'adjusted' ratio of proceeds to prime costs, k', is the same series as in Table 3 above. For the original values of the ratio of the materials bill to the wage bill and for the description of the calculation of the 'adjusted' series j' given in Table 5, see Statistical Appendix, Notes 2 and 3. The adjustments introduced for changes in the scope and methods of the Census are also described there.

of wages in the value added w: indeed, the latter fell more than its adjusted value w'.

No data exist with respect to the relative share of wages in the national income of the United States over a long period. Such data, however, are available for the United Kingdom. In Table 7, the relative share of wages in the national home-produced income[1] of the United Kingdom is given. The table includes in addition the ratio of the Sauerbeck index of wholesale prices to the index of wage rates which can be taken as an

Table 7. Relative Share of Wages in the Home-Produced National Income of the United Kingdom, 1881–1924

Period	Relative share of wages	Ratio of Sauerbeck index of wholesale prices to index of wage rates
	(in percentages)	(1881 = 100)
1881–1885	40·0	93·6
1886–1890	40·5	80·8
1891–1895	41·7	73·5
1896–1900	40·7	70·6
1901–1905	39·8	72·4
1906–1910	37·9	78·3
1911–1913	37·1	82·1
1924	40·6	69·6

Source: A. R. Prest, 'National Income of the United Kingdom,' Economic Journal, March 1948; Unpublished estimates of U.K. income from overseas by F. Hilgerdt; Statist; A. L. Bowley, Wages and Income in the United Kingdom Since 1860, Table 1, p. 6, Woods' index of wage rates.

approximate indicator of changes in the ratio of prices of raw materials to unit wage costs. Although the Sauerbeck index is a general index of wholesale prices, it is based mainly on prices of raw materials and semi-manufactures. It is true that the index of wage rates rises more quickly (or falls more slowly) than the index of wage costs, due to the secular increase in productivity, and thus a decreasing trend is involved in our indicator of the ratio of raw material prices to unit wage costs.

[1] Home-produced national income is national income exclusive of income from foreign investments which is irrelevant to the problem of distribution considered here. It should be noticed that even after this adjustment the data do not correspond fully to our concepts because they relate to net rather than to gross national income and because national income includes the income of government employees while we dealt above with the relative share of wages in the income of the private sector. However, it seems probable that these factors could not affect seriously the trend of the relative share of wages in the national income.

However, this trend is likely to be slow, especially since the wage-rate index is partly based on piece rates. It is therefore very likely that the ratio of prices of raw materials to wage costs fell from 1881–1885 to 1891–1895 as did the indicator. It certainly rose from 1896–1900 to 1911–1913; and it fell again from 1911–1913 to 1924.

The movement of the relative share of labour in the national· income may be plausibly interpreted in the following way. While there was a long-run rise in the degree of monopoly, its influence was largely offset by the fall in the ratio of raw material prices to unit wage costs from 1881–1885 to 1891–1895. The influence of the degree of monopoly was reinforced by the rise of the ratio of raw material prices to unit wage costs in the period 1896–1900 to 1911–1913, and finally more than offset by a fall in this ratio from 1911–1913 to 1924. Thus, the fact that the relative share of wages in the national income was about the same in 1924 as in 1881–1885, would be, according to this interpretation, the result of the accidental balancing of the influence of changes in the degree of monopoly and changes in the ratio of raw material prices to unit wage costs. Unfortunately, this interpretation cannot be considered conclusive because of the possible influence of changes in the industrial composition of national income.

Changes in the relative share of wages in the value added of United States manufacturing during the Great Depression

In Table 8 changes in the relative share of wages in the value added of United States manufacturing during the Great Depression are analysed by employing the same method as that used for the analysis of long-run changes. (Cf. Table 6.) The table contains the 'adjusted' ratio of proceeds to prime costs k', and the 'adjusted' ratio of the material bill to the wage bill j'.

From k' and j' is calculated w'—the 'adjusted' relative share of wages in the value added—by means of formula (3'). Finally, the actual relative share of wages in the value added, w, is given. The changes in the difference $w-w'$ reflect the effect of changes in industrial composition.

If we abstract tentatively from the influence of changes in industrial composition, and thus take into consideration only k', j' and w', the following picture emerges. From 1929 to 1933

Table 8. Relative Share of Wages in Value Added in Manufacturing in the United States, 1929–1937

Year	Ratio of proceeds to prime costs	Ratio of materials bill to wage bill	Share of wages in value added	Share of wages in value added
	Assuming stable industrial composition (base year 1929)			Original data
	k'	j'	w'	w
	(in percentages)			
1929	139·4	346	36·2	36·2
1931	142·2	307	36·8	35·7
1933	142·3	312	36·4	35·0
1935	136·7	314	39·7	37·9
1937	136·6	331	38·8	38·6

Source: United States Census of Manufactures. For details see Statistical Appendix, Notes 2 and 3.

the ratio of proceeds to prime costs, k', increases, reflecting the rise in the degree of monopoly during a depression (cf. p. 23). However, at the same time the ratio of the materials bill to the wage bill declines as a result of the fall, typical for a slump, in the prices of raw materials in relation to wages. The influence of these two factors upon the relative share of wages in the value added, w', is in opposite directions. As w' was stable from 1929 to 1933 it appears that these two factors were in balance. From 1933 to 1937 the 'adjusted' relative share of wages in the value added, w', increased as a result of the fall in the 'adjusted' ratio of proceeds to prime costs, k', which was not offset by the rise in the 'adjusted' ratio of the materials bill to the wage bill, j'. This situation reflects the relatively great reduction in the degree of monopoly in the recovery resulting from the increased power of trade unions. The long-run tendency for prices of raw materials to fall relative to wage costs, which is reflected in the fact that j' did not recover in 1937 to its 1929 level, was a contributory factor.

As to the difference between the actual and 'adjusted' relative share of wages in the value added, $w-w'$, it appears that it fell in the depression (w fell somewhat from 1929 to 1933, while w' remained roughly stable; from 1933 to 1937 w increased a little more than w'.) This is mainly due to the greater decline in production of investment goods than in total manufacturing production during the slump. Indeed, the relative share of wages in the value added is higher for these goods than for manu-

35

factured goods as a whole and thus the reduction in the importance of the output of investment goods during a depression tends to reduce the relative share of wages in the value added of manufacturing as a whole.

It is of some interest to establish the weight of the three factors considered above in determining the movement of the relative share of wages in the value added during the course of the cycle. For this purpose we may calculate from formula (3′) what the value of w' would be in 1933 if only the ratio of proceeds to prime costs changed while the ratio of the materials bill to the wage bill remained at its 1929 level. The result is 34·6 per cent. This figure, together with the value of w in 1929 and 1933 and the value of w' in 1933 (cf. Table 8), enables us to construct Table 9.

Table 9. Analysis of Changes in the Relative Share of Wages in Value Added in Manufacturing in the United States from 1929 to 1933

Item	Relevant years			
Proceeds ÷ prime costs	1929	1933	1933	1933
Materials bill ÷ wage bill	1929	1929	1933	1933
Industrial composition	1929	1929	1929	1933
Relative share of wages in value added	36·2	34·6	36·4	35·0
Difference		−1·6	+1·8	−1·4

The difference between the second and the first columns gives the effect of the change in the ratio of proceeds to prime costs; that between the third and second columns the effect of the change in the ratio of the materials bill to the wage bill; and that between the fourth and the third columns the effect of the change in the industrial composition.

It will be seen that the effects of the three factors considered are relatively small. Thus, their balance is also small and this accounts for the approximate stability of the relative share of wages in the value added during the depression.

Changes in the relative share of wages in the national income in the United States and the United Kingdom during the Great Depression

Unfortunately, no exact data exist on this subject for the United States because national income statistics do not give wages separately from salaries. It is possible, however, to form an approximate idea about changes in the relative share of wages in the gross income of the private sector for the period 1929–1937. The data on wages in manufacturing industries are available.[1] As mentioned above, wage payments are negligible in some industrial groups, namely in trade (shop assistants being classified as salary earners), finance and real estate, communications and public utilities. For the remaining industries, namely agriculture, mining, construction, transport, and services, only salaries and wages combined are available. If we now calculate a weighted index of wages in manufacturing on the one hand and of salaries and wages in agriculture, mining, construction, transport, and services on the other, we obtain an approximation to the index of the total wage bill. (Indeed, wages in manufacturing constitute about a half of total wages, while salaries in the remaining industries under consideration move to some extent parallel with wages.) We further divide this index by that of the gross income of the private sector and in this way obtain an approximate index of the relative share of wages in this income.

Table 10. **Approximation to the Index of Relative Share of Wages in Gross Income of the Private Sector in the United States, 1929–1937**

Year	Index of wages in manufacturing	Index of wages and salaries in agriculture, mining, construction, transport, and services	Combined index
	In relation to gross income of the private sector		
1929	100·0	100·0	100·0
1930	94·1	105·3	99·7
1931	90·8	109·5	100·1
1932	87·6	113·9	100·8
1933	100·2	109·3	104·8
1934	107·8	102·7	105·3
1935	106·7	96·2	101·5
1936	110·8	99·3	105·1
1937	116·4	96·7	106·6

Source: United States Census of Manufactures, Department of Commerce, National Income Supplement to Survey of Current Business, 1951. *For details see Statistical Appendix, Note 4.*

[1] The series of payrolls is available for all years; it agrees with the Census of Manufactures for the Census years.

This series shows a slow upward long-run trend which can be attributed mainly to a fall in the degree of monopoly as a result of the strengthening of trade unions after 1933 and to some extent to a decline in prices of raw materials in relation to wage costs. The cyclical fluctuations are obviously small. (If salaries in agriculture, mining, construction, transportation, and services were eliminated, the index would be somewhat lower during the depression because salaries in general fall somewhat less than wages; but there is no doubt that the cyclical fluctuations would remain small.) This result is most likely due to the interaction of the same factors which emerged from the analysis of the relative share of wages in the value added of manufacturing industries.

During the depression there was probably a rise in the degree of monopoly in the 'wage-paying' industries, but a fall in the prices of raw materials in relation to wages. The changes in the industrial composition of the private sector during the slump tended to reduce the relative share of wages. Indeed, there was a relative shift in the distribution of national income from 'wage-paying' industries to other industries; and also within the 'wage-paying' group from industries with a higher relative share to those with a lower relative share of wages in gross income. These shifts were due mainly to the relatively greater reduction during the depression of investment activity. Thus, as in the manufacturing industries, the adverse effect of the rise in the degree of monopoly and of the change in industrial composition upon the relative share of wages in the gross income during the depression, appears to have been roughly offset by the influence of the fall of prices of raw materials in relation to wages.

We may now consider the relation between wages and home-produced national income in the United Kingdom in the period 1929–1938.[1] There are available two national income series for the period in question; one estimated by Professor A. L. Bowley and the other by Mr. J. R. S. Stone. However, there exists only the Bowley estimate of the wage bill. Fortunately, however, the

[1] As mentioned above (see footnote to p. 33), the United Kingdom series of home-produced national income does not correspond exactly to the concept of gross income of the private sector used by us since the national income is net of depreciation and includes salaries of government officials. It appears, however, that in the period considered the changes in the relative share of wages in the national income thus defined are indicative of the changes corresponding to our concept.

indices of both variants of national income are in general very similar in the period in question although their absolute values differ.

Table 11. Indices of Relative Share of Wages in National Income in the United Kingdom, 1929–1938

Year	Wage bill (*Bowley*) in relation to national income (*Bowley*)	Wage bill (*Bowley*) in relation to national income (*Stone*)
1929	100·0	100·0
1930	97·6	100·0
1931	98·4	98·8
1932	99·8	99·1
1933	95·3	96·8
1934	96·9	98·5
1935	96·8	98·0
1936	96·7	97·5
1937	102·4	97·9
1938	98·1	97·4

Source: A. L. Bowley, Studies in the National Income; *A. R. Prest, 'National Income of the United Kingdom,'* Economic Journal, *March* 1948; Board of Trade Journal.

In Table 11 are given the indices of the ratios of the wage bill (as estimated by Bowley) to the two variants of national income. It will be seen that both series display no marked cyclical fluctuations.

Cyclical changes in the relative share of wages and salaries in the gross income of the private sector

We have dealt above only with changes in the relative share of wages in aggregate income. We shall now consider briefly the problem of the relative share of labour as a whole in the gross income of the private sector by taking into account not only wages but salaries as well. The application of the theory of income distribution to the analysis of long-run changes in the relative share of wages and salaries in income would be difficult because of the growing importance of salaries in the sum of overheads and profits as a result of increasing concentration of business. However, cyclical fluctuations in the relative share of wages and salaries in the gross income of the private sector can be examined and are of considerable interest.

We have seen above that the relative share of wages in the

gross income of the private sector tends to be fairly stable in the course of the cycle. This cannot be expected, however, for the relative share of wages and salaries combined. Salaries, because of their 'overhead' character, are likely to fall less during the depression and to rise less during the boom than wages. Thus the 'real' wage and salary bill, V, can be expected to fluctuate less during the course of the cycle than the 'real' gross income of the private sector, Y.[1] Consequently, we can write:

$$V = \alpha Y + B$$

where B is a positive constant in the short period although subject to long-run changes. The coefficient α is less than 1 because $V < Y$ and $B > 0$. If we now divide both sides of this equation by the 'real' income Y we obtain

$$\frac{V}{Y} = \alpha + \frac{B}{Y} \tag{4}$$

where $\frac{V}{Y}$ is the relative share of wages and salaries in the gross income of the private sector. $\frac{V}{Y}$ increases, of course, when the 'real' income Y declines. It may be noticed here that equation (4) constitutes one link in the theory of the business cycle developed below.

We now shall apply equation (4) to the United States data for the period 1929–1941. The relative share of wages and salaries[2] in the gross income of the private sector and the value of this income at 1939 prices are given in Table 12.[3] In accordance with equation (4) we correlate the relative share of wages and salaries in income $\frac{V}{Y}$ with the reciprocal of 'real' income $\frac{1}{Y}$ and also with time t to allow for possible secular trend. (t is counted in years from 1935, which is the middle point of the period.) We obtain the following regression equation:

$$\frac{V}{Y} \cdot 100 = 42 \cdot 5 + \frac{707}{Y} + 0 \cdot 11 t$$

[1] We imagine both the wage and salary bill and the gross income of the private sector to be deflated by the same price index.
[2] It should be noticed that in salaries are included those of higher business executives which are rather akin to profits.
[3] As a deflator, the index implicit in the deflation of the real gross product of the private sector by the United States Department of Commerce was used. For details see Statistical Appendix, Notes 5 and 6.

The double correlation coefficient is $0 \cdot 926$. The value of $\dfrac{V}{Y}$ calculated from the regression equation is given in Table 12 as well. The positive trend probably reflects the influence of the fall in the degree of monopoly and in the prices of raw materials in relation to unit wage costs.

Table 12. Relative Share of Wages and Salaries in Gross Income of the Private Sector in the United States, 1929–1941

Year	Relative share of wages and salaries in gross income of the private sector $\dfrac{V}{Y} \cdot 100$ (in percentages)	Gross income of the private sector at 1939 prices Y (Billion dollars)	Calculated relative share of wages and salaries in gross income of the private sector (in percentages)
1929	50·0	74·1	51·0
1930	52·4	65·9	52·6
1931	55·0	59·3	54·1
1932	57·9	48·0	57·0
1933	57·8	46·9	57·1
1934	56·0	51·9	55·8
1935	52·7	57·7	54·5
1936	53·4	65·5	53·2
1937	53·3	69·0	52·6
1938	53·2	64·3	54·2
1939	53·5	68·8	53·6
1940	52·1	75·9	52·3
1941	51·4	89·6	51·0

Source: United States Department of Commerce, National Income Supplement to Survey of Current Business, 1951.

Part 2

Determination of Profits and National Income

3

The Determinants of Profits

Theory of profits in a simplified model[1]

We may consider first the determinants of profits in a closed economy in which both government expenditure and taxation are negligible. Gross national product will thus be equal to the sum of gross investment (in fixed capital and inventories) and consumption. The value of gross national product will be divided between workers and capitalists, virtually nothing being paid in taxes. The income of workers consists of wages and salaries. The income of capitalists or gross profits includes depreciation and undistributed profits, dividends and withdrawals from unincorporated business, rent and interest. We thus have the following balance sheet of the gross national product, in which we distinguish between capitalists' consumption and workers' consumption:

Gross profits	Gross investment
Wages and salaries	Capitalists' consumption
	Workers' consumption
Gross national product	**Gross national product**

If we make the additional assumption that workers do not save, then workers' consumption is equal to their income. It follows directly then:

Gross profits = Gross investment + capitalists' consumption

What is the significance of this equation? Does it mean that profits in a given period determine capitalists' consumption and investment, or the reverse of this? The answer to this question

[1] The theory of profits given here was developed back in 1935 in my 'Essai d'une Théorie de Mouvement Cyclique des Affaires,' *Revue d'Economie Politique*, Mars–Avril 1935, and my 'A Macrodynamic Theory of Business Cycles,' *Econometrica*, July 1935.

depends on which of these items is directly subject to the decisions of capitalists. Now, it is clear that capitalists may decide to consume and to invest more in a given period than in the preceding one, but they cannot decide to earn more. It is, therefore, their investment and consumption decisions which determine profits, and not vice versa.

If the period which we consider is short, we may say that the capitalists' investment and consumption are determined by decisions shaped in the *past*. For the execution of investment orders takes a certain time, and capitalists' consumption responds to changes in the factors which influence it only with a certain delay.

If capitalists always decided to consume and to invest in a given period what they had earned in the preceding period, the profits in the given period would be equal to those in the preceding one. In such a case profits would remain stationary, and the problem of interpreting the above equation would lose its importance. But such is *not* the case. Although profits in the preceding period are one of the important determinants of capitalists' consumption and investment, capitalists in general do *not* decide to consume and invest in a given period precisely what they have earned in the preceding one. This explains why profits are *not* stationary, but fluctuate in time.

The above argument requires certain qualifications. Past investment decisions may not fully determine the volume of investment in a given period, owing to unexpected accumulation or running down of stocks. The importance of this factor, however, seems to have been frequently exaggerated.

A second qualification arises out of the fact that consumption and investment decisions will usually be made in real terms, and in the meantime prices may change. For instance, a piece of ordered capital equipment may now cost more than at the time when the order was given. To get over this difficulty both sides of the equation will be assumed to be calculated at constant prices.

We may now conclude that the real gross profits in a given short period are determined by decisions of capitalists with respect to their consumption and investment shaped in the past, subject to correction for unexpected changes in the volume of stocks.

For the understanding of the problems considered it is useful

46

to present the above from a somewhat different angle. Imagine that following the Marxian 'schemes of reproduction' we subdivide all the economy into three departments: department I producing investment goods, department II producing consumption goods for capitalists, and department III producing consumption goods for workers. The capitalists in department III, after having sold to workers the amount of consumption goods corresponding to their wages, will still have left a surplus of consumption goods which will be the equivalent of their profits. These goods will be sold to the workers of department I and department II, and as the workers do not save it will be equal to their incomes. Thus, total profits will be equal to the sum of profits in department I, profits in department II, and wages in these two departments: or, total profits will be equal to the value of production of these two departments—in other words, to the value of production of investment goods and consumption goods for capitalists.

The production of department I and department II will also determine the production of department III if the distribution between profits and wages in all departments is given. The production of department III will be pushed up to the point where profits earned out of that production will be equal to the wages of departments I and II. Or, to put it differently, employment and production of department III will be pushed up to the point where the surplus of this production over what the workers of this department buy with their wages is equal to the wages of departments I and II.

The above clarifies the role of the 'distribution factors,' i.e. factors determining the distribution of income (such as degree of monopoly) in the theory of profits. Given that profits are determined by capitalists' consumption and investment, it is the workers' income (equal here to workers' consumption) which is determined by the 'distribution factors.' In this way capitalists' consumption and investment conjointly with the 'distribution factors' determine the workers' consumption and consequently the national output and employment. The national output will be pushed up to the point where profits carved out of it in accordance with the 'distribution factors' are equal to the sum of capitalists' consumption and investment.[1]

1 The above argument is based on the assumption of elastic supply which was made in Part I. However, if the output of consumption goods for workers is at

47

The general case

We may now pass from our simplified model to the real situation where the economy is not a closed system and where government expenditure and taxation are not negligible. The gross national product is then equal to the sum of gross investment, consumption, government expenditure on goods and services, and the surplus of exports over imports. ('Investment' here stands for private investment, public investment being included in government expenditure on goods and services.) Since the total value of production is divided between capitalists and workers or paid in taxes, the value of gross national product on the income side will be equal to gross profits net of taxes, wages and salaries net of taxes, plus all taxes direct and indirect. We thus have the following balance sheet of the gross national product:

Gross profits	Gross investment
net of (direct) taxes	Export surplus
Wages and salaries	Government expenditure on
net of (direct) taxes	goods and services
Taxes (direct and indirect)	Capitalists' consumption
	Workers' consumption
Gross national product	**Gross national product**

Part of the taxes are spent on transfers such as social benefits, while the remaining part serves to finance government expenditure on goods and services. Let us subtract from both sides of the balance sheet, taxes minus transfers. On the income side the item 'Taxes' will disappear and we shall add transfers to wages and salaries. On the other side, the difference between government expenditure on goods and services and taxes minus transfers will be equal to the budget deficit. Thus, the balance sheet will be as follows:

Gross profits	Gross investment
net of taxes	Export surplus
Wages, salaries and	Budget deficit
transfers net of taxes	Capitalists' consumption
	Workers' consumption
Gross national products	**Gross national product**
minus taxes plus transfers	**minus taxes plus transfers**

capacity level any increase in capitalists' consumption or investment will merely cause a rise in prices of these goods. In such a case it is the rise in prices of consumption goods for workers which will increase profits in department III up to a point where they are equal to the higher amount of wages in departments I and II. Real wage rates will fall, reflecting the fact that an increased wage bill meets an unchanged supply of consumption goods.

By subtracting now from both sides wages, salaries and transfers net of taxes, we obtain the following equation:

$$\text{Gross profits net of taxes} = \begin{cases} \text{Gross investment} \\ + \text{ Export surplus} \\ + \text{ Budget deficit} \\ - \text{ Workers' saving} \\ + \text{ Capitalists' consumption} \end{cases}$$

Thus, this equation differs from the equation of the simplified model in that instead of investment we have now investment plus export surplus plus budget deficit minus workers' saving. It is clear, however, that our previous relationship still obtains if we assume that both the budget and foreign trade are balanced and that the workers do not save, that is:

Gross profits after tax = Gross investment + capitalists' consumption

Even if these assumptions are made, the system is much more realistic than in the first simplified model and all of the arguments of the previous section still apply. It has to be remembered, however, that we are dealing now with profits after tax, while in the first simplified model the problem did not arise because taxes were assumed to be negligible.

Savings and investment

Let us subtract on both sides of the general equation for profits (see top of this page) capitalists' consumption and add workers' savings. We obtain:

Capitalists' gross savings	Gross investment
Workers' savings	Export surplus
	Budget deficit
Total gross savings	**Total gross savings**

Thus, total savings are equal to the sum of private investment, export surplus and budget deficit, while capitalists' savings are, of course, equal to this sum minus workers' savings.

If we now assume that both foreign trade and the government budget are balanced we obtain:

Gross savings = Gross investment

If we assume, moreover, that workers do not save we have:

Capitalists' gross savings = Gross investment

This equation is equivalent to:

Gross profits = Gross investment + Capitalists' consumption

because it may be obtained from the latter equation by the deduction of capitalists' consumption from both sides.

It should be emphasized that the equality between savings and investment plus export surplus plus budget deficit in the general case—or investment alone in the special case—will be valid under all circumstances. In particular, it will be independent of the level of the rate of interest which was customarily considered in economic theory to be the factor equilibrating the demand for and supply of new capital. In the present conception investment, once carried out, automatically provides the savings necessary to finance it. Indeed, in our simplified model, profits in a given period are the direct outcome of capitalists' consumption and investment in that period. If investment increases by a certain amount, savings out of profits are *pro tanto* higher.

To put it in a more concrete fashion: if some capitalists increase their investment by using for this purpose their liquid reserves, the profits of other capitalists will rise *pro tanto* and thus the liquid reserves invested will pass into the possession of the latter. If additional investment is financed by bank credit, the spending of the amounts in question will cause equal amounts of saved profits to accumulate as bank deposits. The investing capitalists will thus find it possible to float bonds to the same extent and thus to repay the bank credits.

One important consequence of the above is that the rate of interest cannot be determined by the demand for and supply of new capital because investment 'finances itself.' The factors determining the level of the rate of interest are discussed in Part III below.

The effect of the export surplus and budget deficit

In what follows we shall frequently assume a balanced government budget and balanced foreign trade, as well as zero workers' savings, which will enable us to base our argument on the equality between profits after taxes and the sum of gross investment and capitalists' consumption. It is useful, however, to say a few words now about the significance of the influence of the export surplus and the budget deficit on profits.

According to the formula established above, profits are equal to investment plus export surplus plus budget deficit minus workers' savings plus capitalists' consumption. It follows directly that an increase in the export surplus will raise profits *pro tanto* if other components are unchanged. The mechanism involved is the same as that described on p. 47. The value of an increment in the production of the export sector will be accounted for by the increase in profits and wages of that sector. The wages, however, will be spent on consumption goods. Thus, production of consumption goods for workers will be expanded up to the point where profits out of this production will increase by the amount of additional wages in the export sector.[1]

It follows directly from the above that the export surplus enables profits to increase above that level which would be determined by capitalists' investment and consumption. It is from this point of view that the fight for foreign markets may be viewed. The capitalists of a country which manages to capture foreign markets from other countries are able to increase their profits at the expense of the capitalists of the other countries. Similarly, a colonial metropolis may achieve an export surplus through investment in its dependencies.[2]

A budget deficit has an effect similar to that of an export surplus. It also permits profits to increase above the level determined by private investment and capitalists' consumption. In a sense the budget deficit can be considered as an artificial export surplus. In the case of the export surplus a country receives more for its exports than it pays for its imports. In the case of the budget deficit the private sector of the economy receives more from government expenditure than it pays in taxes. The counterpart of the export surplus is an increase in the indebtedness of the foreign countries towards the country considered. The counterpart of the budget deficit is an increase in the indebtedness of the government towards the private sector.

[1] If the production of consumption goods for workers is at capacity level, prices of these goods will rise up to a point where profits out of this production will increase by the amount of additional wages in the export sector (cf. footnote to p. 47).

[2] Foreign lending by a given country need not be associated with exports of goods from that country. If a country *A* lends to country *B*, the latter can spend the proceeds of the loan in country *C*, which may increase *pro tanto* its stock of gold and liquid foreign assets. In this case foreign lending by country *A* will cause an export surplus in country *C* accompanied by an accumulation of gold or liquid foreign assets in that country. In the case of colonial dependencies, this situation is not apt to arise, i.e. the amount invested will be normally spent in the metropolis.

Both of these surpluses of receipts over payments generate profits in the same way.

The above shows clearly the significance of 'external' markets (including those created by budget deficits) for a capitalist economy. Without such markets profits are conditioned by the ability of capitalists to consume or to undertake capital investment. It is the export surplus and the budget deficit which enable the capitalists to make profits over and above their own purchases of goods and services.

The connection between 'external' profits and imperalism is obvious. The fight for the division of existing foreign markets and the expansion of colonial empires, which provide new opportunities for export of capital associated with export of goods, can be viewed as a drive for export surplus, the classical source of 'external' profits. Armaments and wars, usually financed by budget deficits, are also a source of this kind of profits.

4

Profits and Investment

Profits and investment under simplifying assumptions

It was noted above (p. 46) that capitalists' investment and consumption are determined by decisions shaped in the *past*. The determinants of investment decisions which are rather complex in character are considered in Chapter 9 below. We shall deal here with the determination of capitalists' consumption.

We may make the following assumption, which is plausible as a first approximation, about the 'real' capitalists' consumption in a given year, C_t: that it consists of a stable part A and a part proportionate to $P_{t-\lambda}$, the real profits after tax of some time ago; that is:

$$C_t = qP_{t-\lambda} + A \qquad (5)$$

where λ indicates the delay of the reaction of capitalists' consumption to the change in their current income. q is positive and < 1 because capitalists tend to consume only a part of the increment in income. In fact, this part is likely to be rather small so that q is probably considerably less than 1. Finally, A is a constant in the short run although subject to long-run changes. We shall assume for the time being that foreign trade and the government budget are balanced and that workers do not save. In this case profits after tax P are equal to the sum of investment I and capitalists' consumption C:

$$P = I + C \qquad (6)$$

Substituting the value of C from equation (5) we obtain:

$$P_t = I_t + qP_{t-\lambda} + A \qquad (7)$$

It follows that 'real' profits at time t are determined by current investment and profits at the time $t - \lambda$. Profits at the time

$t - \lambda$ will be in turn determined by investment at that time and by profits at the time $t - 2\lambda$, and so on. It is thus clear that profits at time t are a linear function of investment at time t, $t - \lambda$, $t - 2\lambda$, etc., and that the coefficients of investment I_t, $I_{t-\lambda}$, $I_{t-2\lambda}$, etc. in this relation will be $1, q, q^2$, etc., respectively. Now q, as said above, is less than 1 and probably considerably less than 1. Thus the series of coefficients $1, q, q^2, \ldots$ will be quickly decreasing and consequently among I_t, $I_{t-\lambda}$, $I_{t-2\lambda}$, $\ldots$ only those relatively near in time will count in the determination of profits, P_t. Profits will thus be a function both of current investment and of investment in the near past; or, roughly speaking, profits follow investment with a time lag. We can thus write as an approximate equation:

$$P_t = f(I_{t-\omega}) \qquad (8)$$

where ω is the time lag involved.

The shape of the function f can be determined as follows. Let us go back for a moment to equation (7) and substitute for P its value from equation (8):

$$f(I_{t-\omega}) = I_t + qf(I_{t-\omega-\lambda}) + A$$

This equation should be fulfilled whatever the course in time of investment I_t. Thus, it should cover *inter alia* the case where investment is maintained for some time at a stable level so that we have $I_t = I_{t-\omega} = I_{t-\omega-\lambda}$. It follows:

$$f(I_t) = I_t + qf(I_t) + A$$

or
$$f(I_t) = \frac{I_t + A}{1 - q}$$

As this equality is fulfilled for any level of I_t it gives us the shape of the function f. We thus can write the equation (8) as:

$$P_t = \frac{I_{t-\omega} + A}{1 - q} \qquad (8')$$

The significance of equation (8') is in that it reduces the number of determinants of profits from two to one as a result of taking into consideration the dependence of capitalists' consumption on past profits as given by equation (5). Profits according to equation (8') are determined fully by investment with a certain time lag being involved. Moreover, investment

54

depends on investment decisions still farther back in time. It follows that profits are determined by past investment decisions.

The interpretation of equation (8′) may give rise to certain difficulties. Under the given assumptions that foreign trade and the government budget are balanced and that workers do not save, investment is equal to capitalists' savings (see p. 49). It thus follows directly from equation (8′) that capitalists' savings 'lead' profits. This result may appear paradoxical. 'Common sense' would suggest the opposite sequence—namely, that savings are determined by profits. This, however, is not the case. Capitalists' consumption in a certain period is the result of their decisions based on past profits. Since profits usually change in the meantime, actual savings do *not* correspond to the intended disposition of income. Indeed, actual savings which are equal to investment *will* 'lead' profits as shown by equation (8′). How this happens may be illustrated by the following example. Imagine that for some time both investment and thus savings and also profits are constant. Imagine that there is a sudden change in investment. Savings will increase immediately together with investment, and profits will rise by the same amount. However, capitalists' consumption will rise only after some time as a result of this primary increase in profits. Thus, profits will still be increasing after the rise in investment and savings has already come to a stop.

The general case

How will equation (8′) change if we do *not* postulate that foreign trade and the government budget are balanced and that workers' savings are zero? If we denote the sum of private investment, exports surplus and budget deficit by I', workers' savings by s and capitalists' consumption as above by C, we have for profits the equation (see p. 49):

$$P = I' - s + C$$

It will be seen that for this general case equation (8′) will be modified to:

$$P_t = \frac{I'_{t-\omega} - s_{t-\omega} + A}{1 - q} \tag{8''}$$

Indeed, the formula (8′) was obtained from the relation between capitalists' consumption and profits (equation 5) and from the

55

assumption that investment I is equal to the difference between profits and capitalists' consumption. Thus, when this difference is equal to $I' - s$, it is this item that should replace I in formula (8').

Equation (8'') may be replaced by a simpler although approximate formula. It should be remembered that total savings are equal to the sum of investment, export surplus and budget deficit, I' (see p. 49). Further, although in general workers' savings, s, are not equal to zero, their level and absolute changes are small as compared with total savings. Moreover, s must show in the course of the business cycle a pronounced correlation with total savings. (This follows from our considerations in the next chapter which establish a relation between profits and national income.) Thus, $I' - s$ must be closely correlated with I'. We have consequently as a good approximation:

$$P_t = \frac{I'_{t-\omega} + A'}{1 - q'} \tag{8'''}$$

where the change of parameters from q to q' and from A to A' reflects the replacement of $I'_{t-\omega} - s_{t-\omega}$ by a linear function of $I'_{t-\omega}$. It should be remembered that q is a coefficient indicating what part of an increment in profit will be devoted to consumption while the constant A is that part of capitalists' consumption which is stable in the short-run although subject to long-run changes. q' and A' reflect in addition the relation of workers' savings to total savings which are equal to I'.

The formula (8''') is superior to formula (8'') in that it may be illustrated statistically. This is virtually impossible for (8'') because no statistical data about workers' savings, s, are available.

Statistical illustration

We shall apply equation (8''') to the United States data for the period 1929–1940. The 'real' values of gross profits after tax, P,[1] and of I' are given in Table 13. The meaning of I' is slightly modified as compared with its basic concept. In addition to gross investment, export surplus and budget deficit, it here includes brokerage fees. In the United States statistics these are

---

[1] P is obtained from gross profits by deducting all direct taxes. *Direct* taxes on wages and salaries were very small in the period considered.

included in consumption. However, as this is a typical capital expenditure which is not closely related to income, it is proper here to consider it on a par with investment. As a deflator for both series the price index implicit in the deflation of gross national product of the private sector is used.[1]

Table 13. Determination of Profits in the United States, 1929–1940

Year	Gross profits after taxes	Gross private investment plus export surplus plus budget deficit plus brokerage fees		Calculated gross profits after taxes
	P_t	I'_t	$I'_{t-\frac{1}{4}}$	
		(Billions of dollars at 1939 prices)		
1929	33·7	14·2	13·7	33·2
1930	28·5	10·2	11·2	29·6
1931	24·5	5·5	6·7	23·3
1932	18·3	3·2	3·8	19·2
1933	17·6	3·4	3·3	18·2
1934	20·4	6·0	5·3	20·6
1935	24·4	8·4	7·8	23·7
1936	26·8	11·6	10·8	27·5
1937	27·9	10·8	10·6	26·9
1938	26·2	9·0	9·5	25·2
1939	28·1	12·9	11·9	28·2
1940	31·0	15·9	15·1	32·2

Source: Department of Commerce, National Income Supplement to Survey of Current Business, 1951.

Before establishing the correlation between P and I' it was necessary to determine the time lag, ω. This was complicated by the fact that some trend also appeared to be involved in the relation between P and I'. In order to circumvent this difficulty, the trend was approximately eliminated by taking into consideration the first differences ΔP and $\Delta I'$. From correlating these differences it appeared that the best fit is obtained for a time lag of about three months.

In view of this, P was correlated with $I'_{t-\frac{1}{4}}$, i.e. with I' shifted three months back by means of interpolation. Thus, $I'_{t-\frac{1}{4}}$ was obtained by taking three-fourths of I' in a given year and one-fourth of I' in the preceding year. To allow for trend a double correlation was established of P with $I'_{t-\frac{1}{4}}$ and the time t

[1] For details of the calculation of P and I' see Statistical Appendix, Notes 7 and 8.

(counted in years from the middle of the period 1929–1940, i.e. from the beginning of 1935). The regression equation is:

$$P_t = 1 \cdot 34 I'_{t-\frac{1}{4}} + 13 \cdot 4 - 0 \cdot 13t$$

The value of profits calculated from this equation are given for comparison with actual profits in Table 13. The correlation is very close. The double correlation coefficient is $0 \cdot 986$.

If there were no saving out of wages and salaries the coefficient of $I'_{t-\frac{1}{4}}$ would be equal $\dfrac{1}{1-q}$ in equation (8''). In this case we should have for q, which is the coefficient indicating what part of an increment of profits will be directed to consumption:

$$\frac{1}{1-q} = 1 \cdot 34; \quad q = 0 \cdot 25$$

This would mean that only 25 per cent of additional profits would be devoted to consumption and 75 per cent to savings. Actually, the coefficient q will be larger, because part of savings comes from labour income. However, q is unlikely to exceed 30 per cent by very much.

The trend coefficient is negative, which is probably mainly accounted for by the fact that, as a result of the Great Depression, profits in the 'thirties were much lower than profits in the preceding decade, and that this long-run fall in profits could have caused a decline in the constant, A, during the period considered. In other words, capitalists' standard of living was declining as a result of the long-run slump in profits.

5

Determination of National Income and Consumption

Introduction

In Chapter 2 the relative share of wages and salaries in the national income was investigated and in the last two chapters the relationship between profits and I', the sum of investment, export surplus and budget deficit was established. The combination of the results of these two inquiries will enable us to establish a relation between the national income and I'. Thus, in the special case where foreign trade and the government budget are balanced, the national income will be related to investment I.

The formula for the relative share of wages and salaries in the gross income of the private sector established in Chapter 2 (p. 40) is as follows:

$$\frac{V}{Y} = \alpha + \frac{B}{Y} \qquad (4)$$

where V is the 'real' wage and salary bill, and Y is the 'real' gross income of the private sector. The coefficient α is positive and < 1 and the constant B which is subject to long-run changes, is also positive. The difference between Y and V is gross profits before taxes π. (In the preceding chapter P represented gross profits *after* taxes.) We thus have:

$$\frac{Y - \pi}{Y} = \alpha + \frac{B}{Y}$$

or:

$$Y = \frac{\pi + B}{1 - \alpha} \qquad (9)$$

59

For an understanding of the subsequent discussion a few words should be added about the difference between the gross *national product* and the gross *income* of the *private sector, Y.* The difference between the gross *national* product and the gross *private* product is accounted for by the government product as measured by payments to government employees. The difference between the value of gross private *product* and the gross *income* of the private sector, *Y,* is accounted for by indirect taxes which are included in the value of the private product.[1] Thus, the difference between gross national product and the gross income of the private sector consists of payments to government employees and indirect taxes.

National product, profits, and investment in a simplified model

We shall discuss the problem of determination of national product or income first with respect to the simplified model considered at the beginning of Chapter 3. We assumed there a closed system and a negligible government revenue and expenditure. As a result gross national product is equal to the sum of private investment and consumption. We also abstracted from workers' savings. For such a model, as we have seen, formula (8') relating profits after taxes, *P,* to investment, *I* (see p. 54), is valid:

$$P_t = \frac{I_{t-\omega} + A}{1 - q} \tag{8'}$$

where $1 > q > 0$ and $A > 0$. Since tax revenue is negligible, profits before and after tax may be taken as identical. Gross national product and gross private income of the private sector, *Y,* may also be taken as identical since both payments to government employees and indirect taxation are negligible. We thus have the following equations for the determination of gross national product:

$$Y_t = \frac{P_t + B}{1 - \alpha} \tag{9'}$$

$$P_t = \frac{I_{t-\omega} + A}{1 - q} \tag{8'}$$

[1] Since the gross income of the private sector, *Y,* is taken here before direct taxation, *Y* includes *direct* taxes.

It is clear that the gross income or product, Y_t, is fully determined by investment, $I_{t-\omega}$.

Since equation (9') reflects the factors determining the distribution of national income we can also say: the gross income, Y_t, is pushed up to a point at which profits out of it, as determined by the 'distribution factors,' correspond to the level of investment $I_{t-\omega}$. The role of the 'distribution factors' is thus to determine income or product on the basis of profits which are in turn determined by investment. The mechanism of such determination of income has already been described in Chapter 3 (see p. 47).

It follows directly that changes in the distribution of income occur not by way of a change in profits, P, but through a change in gross income or product, Y. Imagine, for instance, that as a result of the increase in the degree of monopoly the relative share of profits in the gross income rises. Profits will remain unchanged because they continue to be determined by investment which depends on past investment decisions, but the real wages and salaries and the gross income or product will fall. The level of income or product will decline to the point at which the higher relative share of profits yields the same absolute level of profits. In our equations it will be reflected as follows: the increase in the degree of monopoly will cause a fall of the coefficient, α.[1] As a result, a lower level of income or product, Y_t, will correspond to a given level of investment, $I_{t-\omega}$.

Changes in investment and consumption in a simplified model

Given the relations between profits and investment and gross income and profits, as expressed by equations (8') and (9'), any change in investment causes a definite change in income. A rise in investment by $\Delta I_{t-\omega}$ causes with a time lag a rise in profits by:

$$\Delta P_t = \frac{\Delta I_{t-\omega}}{1-q}$$

Moreover, a rise in profits by ΔP causes a rise in the gross income or product by:

[1] According to equation (4), α is that part of the relative share of wages and salaries in income Y which is independent of the level of Y; the other part $\frac{B}{Y}$ stands for the influence of the overhead element in salaries.

$$\Delta Y_t = \frac{\Delta P_t}{1 - \alpha}$$

or
$$\Delta Y_t = \frac{\Delta I_{t-\omega}}{(1 - \alpha)(1 - q)}$$

It should be remembered that q is the coefficient indicating that part of ΔP, an increment of profits, which will be devoted to consumption; and that α is the coefficient indicating that part of ΔY, an increment in the gross income, which goes to wages and salaries. Both $1 - q$ and $1 - \alpha$ are < 1, so that $\Delta Y_t >$ $\Delta I_{t-\omega}$. In other words, gross income or product increases more than investment owing to the effect of the rise in investment upon capitalists' consumption $\left(\text{factor } \dfrac{1}{1 - q}\right)$ and upon workers' income $\left(\text{factor } \dfrac{1}{1 - \alpha}\right)$. Since workers' consumption is here assumed to be equal to their income, this means that income increases more than investment because of the influence of the increase in investment upon capitalists' and workers' consumption.[1] During a slump the fall in investment also causes a reduction in consumption so that the fall in employment is larger than that arising directly from the curtailment of investment activity.

In order to bring into focus the nature of this process in the capitalist economy it is useful to consider what the effect of a reduction in investment in a socialist system would be. The workers released from the production of investment goods would be employed in consumption goods industries. The increased supply of these goods would be absorbed by means of a reduction in their prices. Since profits of the socialist industries would be equal to investment, prices would have to be reduced to the point where the decline in profits would be equal to the fall in the value of investment. In other words, full employment would be maintained through the reduction of prices in relation to costs. In the capitalist system, however, the price-cost relationship, as reflected in equation (9'), is main-

[1] It should be noticed that equation (9') which reflects the price-cost relationship, is based on the condition of elastic supply postulated in Part I. If the supply of consumption goods is inelastic an increase in investment will not result in a rise in the volume of consumption but merely in an increase in the prices of consumption goods (cf. footnote to p. 47). In the subsequent argument we continue to assume, in line with Part I, the condition of elastic supply.

tained and profits fall by the same amount as investment plus capitalists' consumption through the reduction in output and employment. It is indeed paradoxical that, while the apologists of capitalism usually consider the 'price mechanism' to be the great advantage of the capitalist system, price flexibility proves to be a characteristic feature of the socialist economy.[1]

Up to this point we have been considering the relation between the *absolute* changes of investment, I, profits, P, and gross income or product, Y. It is of interest also to compare their *proportionate* changes. Let us go back for this purpose to equations (8') and (9'). It should be remembered that the constant A, the stable part of capitalists' consumption, and the constant B, the stable part of salaries, are positive. It follows that profits, P, change proportionately less in the course of the business cycle than investment, I, and that the same is true of gross income, Y, in relation to profits, P. Consequently, the relative changes of gross income, Y, are smaller than those of investment, I.

Since in our model gross income or product, Y, is equal to the sum of investment and consumption, the relative changes of consumption are smaller than those of gross income. For, if one component (investment) varies proportionately more than the sum (gross income or product) the other component (consumption) must vary proportionately less than the sum. It follows directly that investment varies proportionately more than consumption, or in other words, that it falls in relation to consumption during the slump and rises during the boom.

The general case

Let us now drop the assumption that government expenditure and revenue are negligible. For the time being we may continue to assume that foreign trade and the government budget are balanced and that workers do not save. Thus, equation (8'):

$$P_t = \frac{I_{t-\omega} + A}{1 - q} \qquad (8')$$

still holds good but profits before taxes, π, are no longer identical with profits after taxes, P. We shall assume that the

---

[1] It should be noticed that in an expanding socialist economy a reduction in the price-cost ratio will reflect a relative rather than an absolute shift from investment to consumption.

tax system is given and that the relation between 'real' profits before taxes, π, and 'real' profits after taxes, P, can be expressed approximately by a linear function. We are then able to substitute for formula (9') the equation:

$$Y_t = \frac{P_t + B'}{1 - \alpha'} \qquad (9'')$$

where the constant α' and B' do not depend merely on the factors underlying the distribution of national income, but are influenced also by the effect of the tax system on profits. From these two equations it is apparent that gross income of the private sector Y is again determined—with a time lag—by investment I. To an increment in investment $\Delta I_{t-\omega}$ there corresponds an increment in gross income:

$$\Delta Y_t = \frac{I_{t-\omega}}{(1 - \alpha')(1 - q)}$$

ΔY is here again larger than ΔI. This, however, is accounted for not only by the increase in capitalists' and workers' consumption following the rise in investment, but also by the larger volume of direct taxes which they pay out of increased income.

Passing now to the general case where foreign trade and the government budget are not necessarily balanced and workers' savings are not necessarily zero, we have (see p. 56):

$$P_t = \frac{I'_{t-\omega} + A'}{1 - q'} \qquad (8''')$$

where I' is the sum of investment, export surplus and budget deficit, and where q' and A' differ from q and A in equation (8') in that they reflect workers' savings. The shape of equation (9'') is unchanged:

$$Y_t = \frac{P_t + B'}{1 - \alpha'} \qquad (9'')$$

These two equations determine Y_t in terms of $I'_{t-\omega}$. The increment in Y_t corresponding to the increment of $I'_{t-\omega}$ is:

$$\Delta Y_t = \frac{\Delta I'_{t-\omega}}{(1 - \alpha')(1 - q')}$$

The determination of consumption is much more complicated than in our simplified model where consumption was the

64

difference between Y and I. In the general case consumption is the difference between aggregate income after tax and savings. Now savings are equal to I', the sum of investment, export surplus and budget deficit. Aggregate income after tax is not equal here to Y. Indeed, the latter is the gross income of the private sector which does not include the income of government employees or government transfer payments and is *before* direct taxes. Aggregate income after tax is equal to Y, plus the income of government employees and government transfer payments and minus all direct taxes. It follows that consumption is equal to $Y - I'$ minus direct taxes, plus income of government employees plus transfers. It is obvious that consumption cannot be fully determined in terms of I' by the above equations which permit the determination of $Y - I'$ only.

Statistical illustration

We shall now estimate the coefficients of the relation between Y and I' for the United States in the period 1929–1941. On p. 40 we established for that period the following equation for the relative share of the wage and salary bill, V, in the gross income of the private sector, Y:

$$\frac{V}{Y} \cdot 100 = 42 \cdot 5 + \frac{707}{Y} + 0 \cdot 11t$$

where the time, t, is counted from 1935.

Taking into consideration that profits before tax $\pi = Y - V$ we obtain

$$\frac{Y - \pi}{Y} = 0 \cdot 425 + \frac{7 \cdot 07}{Y} + 0 \cdot 0011t$$

From this equation Y can be calculated on the basis of π. In Table 14 are given the actual 'real' values of Y and π[1] and the calculated value of Y. The correlation between the actual and calculated Y is extremely close. The coefficient of correlation is $0 \cdot 995$.

If we drop the trend component in the above equation we obtain:

$$Y = 1 \cdot 74\pi + 12 \cdot 2$$

which is the counterpart of equation (9). We still have to take

[1] As deflator, the index implicit in the deflation of the gross product of the private sector by the U.S. Department of Commerce was used again.

Table 14. Gross Income of the Private Sector and Profits in the United States, 1929–1941

Year	Gross income of the private sector Y	Profits before taxes π	Calculated gross income of the private sector
	(Billions of dollars at 1939 prices)		
1929	74·1	37·0	75·5
1930	65·9	31·4	66·2
1931	59·3	26·7	58·2
1932	48·0	20·2	47·0
1933	46·9	19·8	46·2
1934	51·9	22·8	51·6
1935	57·7	27·3	60·0
1936	65·5	30·5	65·2
1937	69·0	32·2	67·9
1938	64·3	30·1	65·7
1939	68·8	32·0	69·0
1940	75·9	36·3	76·1
1941	89·6	43·6	89·0

Source: Department of Commerce, National Income Supplement to Survey of Current Business, 1951. *For details see Statistical Appendix, Notes 6 and 7.*

taxation of profits into consideration if we are to obtain the relation of Y to profits after tax, P. For this purpose we correlate 'real' profits before and after taxes (P was given above in Table 13) and obtain a regression equation which, we may assume, characterizes the tax system prevailing in that period.[1] This relationship between π and P permits us to express Y in terms of profits after tax, P. We thus have as a counterpart of equation (9''):

$$Y_t = 2·03P_t + 10·4$$

The relation between P and I' for the same period was established above (p. 58). Disregarding the trend component we have as a counterpart of equation (8'''):

$$P_t = 1·34\, I'_{t-\frac{1}{4}} + 13·4$$

From these two equations we obtain:

$$Y_t = 2·72\, I'_{t-\frac{1}{4}} + 37·7$$

[1] We take into consideration here the period 1929–1940 rather than 1929–1941. The regression equation is: $P = 0·86\pi + 0·9$. The correlation is quite close which results from the fact that the system of direct taxes was fairly stable over the period considered. Taxes were increased considerably, however, in 1941. (For details see Statistical Appendix, Note 9.)

The increment of Y_t which corresponds, with a time lag, to an increment of $I'_{t-\frac{1}{4}}$ is:

$$\Delta Y_t = 2 \cdot 72 \, \Delta I'_{t-\frac{1}{4}}$$

Thus, *absolute* changes in Y are considerably larger than those in I'. At the same time, according to the preceding equation, *proportionate* changes in Y are smaller than those in I'.

Gross product of the private sector

As stated above (p. 60) the gross income of the private sector, Y, is not equal to the gross product of that sector. In order to pass from the former to the latter it is necessary to add indirect taxes of all kinds, such as excise and custom duties or employers' contributions to social insurance. If we denote the 'real' gross product or output of the private sector by O and the 'real' value of the aggregate indirect taxes by E we have[1]:

$$O = Y + E$$

As was shown above, Y is determined—with a time lag—by the sum of investment, export surplus and budget deficit I' or by investment I if foreign trade and the budget are balanced. In order to determine the gross product of the private sector it is necessary to make some assumptions about E. The relative fluctuations of E in the course of the business cycle are usually much smaller than those of gross income, Y, for the following reasons: (a) indirect taxes are frequently levied on necessities or semi-necessities, the consumption of which fluctuates much less than Y; (b) the rates are frequently fixed in money and not *ad valorem* so that the real value of such rates increases when prices fall. For the sake of simplicity we shall assume in the theory of business cycle developed below that E is a constant.

For the determination of the output of the private sector, O, in terms of the sum of investment, export surplus and budget deficit, I', we now have:

$$O_t = Y_t + E \tag{10}$$

$$Y_t = \frac{P_t + B'}{1 - \alpha'} \tag{9''}$$

$$P_t = \frac{I'_{t-\omega} + A'}{1 - q'} \tag{8'''}$$

---

[1] We imagine Y and E to be deflated by the same price index as O, i.e. by the index of *market* prices.

It follows directly that an increment of $I'_{t-\omega}$ determines an increment of O_t:

$$\Delta O_t = \frac{\Delta I'_{t-\omega}}{(1 - \alpha')(1 - q')}$$

On the assumption that E is a constant, O will show smaller proportionate changes than Y. As the relative changes of Y in the course of the cycle are smaller than those of I' it follows that this is even more true of O. Thus, if foreign trade and the budget are balanced so that $I' = I$, it can be said that the gross product of the private sector O fluctuates less than investment I.

Long-run changes in investment and income

It has been shown above that the relative changes of investment, I (or rather of the sum of investment, export surplus and budget deficit, I', which is equal to savings) in the course of the business cycle are greater than those of gross income or output of the private sector. However, this is not necessarily the case in the long run.

The discrepancy in fluctuations of I' and Y or O in the course of the business cycle depends mainly on two factors: (a) that capitalists' consumption fluctuates less than profits; and (b) that wages plus salaries fluctuate less than gross income, Y. However, capitalists' consumption need not increase more slowly than profits in the course of the long-run growth of an economy. Indeed, the stable part of capitalists' consumption, A (see p. 53), may rise in the long run proportionately with profits, P. In the same way the stable part of wages and salaries, B, which reflects the overhead element in salaries (see p. 40) may also rise in the long run proportionately with income, Y. Thus, in the long run, investment and income may not show disproportionate changes as they do in the course of the business cycle.

It appears that in the United States, in the period 1870–1914, the long-run changes in investment and income were in fact roughly proportional. In Table 15 is given the ratio of 'gross capital formation' to 'gross national income' for that period by decades according to Kuznets. This ratio remained fairly stable.

Although both the numerator and denominator differ in

68

Table 15. Ratio of 'Gross Capital Formation' to 'Gross National Income' in the United States, 1869–1913

(in percentages)

1869–1878	18·9
1874–1883	19·0
1879–1888	19·2
1884–1893	20·8
1889–1898	16·3
1894–1903	21·1
1899–1908	20·1
1904–1913	19·8

Source: S. Kuznets, National Product Since 1869, *New York*, 1946.

concept from I' and Y,[1] it is virtually certain that in the period considered I' and Y moved roughly proportionately to the 'gross capital formation' and to the 'gross national income' respectively. The stability of the ratio of I' to Y does not necessarily mean that both the distribution of income and the proportion of consumption out of profits remained constant because there might have been compensating changes in these factors. In any case the above is not meant to suggest that the long-run stability of the ratio of savings to income is an economic law, but merely to show that there is a possibility of such a relationship.

[1] $I' =$ 'gross capital formation' minus public investment plus budget deficit.
$Y =$ 'gross national income' minus public investment plus budget deficit minus income of government employees.
The differences in question are small in the period considered and therefore proportionality in the change between I' and 'gross capital formation' and between Y and 'gross national income' may be assumed.

Part 3

The Rate of Interest

6

The Short-Term Rate of Interest

Introduction

It has been stated above that the rate of interest cannot be determined by the demand for and the supply of capital because investment automatically brings into existence an equal amount of savings. Thus, investment 'finances itself' whatever the level of the rate of interest (see p. 50). The rate of interest is, therefore, the result of the interplay of other factors. We shall argue that the short-term rate is determined by the value of transactions and the supply of money by banks; and that the long-term rate is determined by anticipations of the short-term rate based on past experience and by estimates of the risk involved in the possible depreciation of long-term assets (see Chapter 7).

Velocity of circulation and the short-term rate

Let M denote the stock of money, i.e. current bank accounts and notes, and T the total turnover, i.e. the aggregate value of transactions in a certain period. T/M is then the velocity of circulation of money, V. It has been frequently assumed that V is constant; and this indeed is the cornerstone of the quantity theory of money. But it seems fairly obvious that the velocity of circulation in fact depends on the short-term rate of interest.

Indeed, the higher the short-term rate the greater is the inducement to invest money for short periods rather than to keep it as cash reserve. Or, to put it more precisely: transactions can be managed with a larger or a smaller stock of money; however, a larger stock of money in relation to turnover means on the average a smoother and more convenient handling of transactions. The higher the short-term rate of interest the more expensive is this convenience as compared with the alternative of investing in short-term assets.[1]

It may be legitimately asked why the short-term rate has been taken into consideration here and not the rate of interest in general. The reason for the singling out of the short-term rate in this context is as follows. The short-term rate of interest is the remuneration for forgoing the convenience of holding cash in its pure form.[2] When holding money is compared with holding short bills, the only difference is that the bill is not directly usable for settling transactions and that it yields interest.[3] When, however, holding money and holding a bond is compared, the risk of a fall in the price of the bond also has to be taken into consideration.[4]

We reached the conclusion above that the velocity of circulation V is an increasing function of the short-term rate of interest ρ or:

$$\frac{T}{M} = V(\rho) \tag{11}$$

It follows directly from this equation that given the function V the short-term rate of interest, ρ, is determined by the value of transactions, T, and the supply of money, M, which, in turn, is determined by banking policy.

The relationship between the short-term rate of interest, ρ, and the velocity of circulation, V, may be represented by a curve with the shape shown in Fig. 3. When V is high, i.e. cash

[1] The question arises here whether in this context, the short-term rate of interest must be understood gross or net of income taxes. If the inconvenience of curtailment of cash holdings is supposed to be finally reflected in a corresponding reduction of profits, then it is the interest gross of taxes which should be taken into account. This seems likely to be the case. However, the results of the subsequent empirical inquiry which relates to the United Kingdom in the period 1930–1938 are not affected by this difficulty since the rate of income tax was fairly stable over that period.

[2] With the qualification that the short-term rate covers in addition some costs and inconveniences involved in investing operations as such or 'investment costs.'

[3] 'Bills' typify here short-term assets in general in which time deposits are also included.

[4] It does not follow from this that any addition to cash at the disposal of a firm will tend to be invested in bills. Imagine that a firm holds cash, bills, and bonds. Imagine further that while its turnover remains unaltered and the short-term and long-term rates of interest are unchanged the firm receives more cash. Now, if the firm invested all the additional cash in bills this would be consistent with the relation between convenience of holding cash and the given short-term rate of interest, but it would unnecessarily reduce the proportion of the relatively 'risky' but more remunerative assets (bonds) in its holdings. Thus, the firm will tend to invest part of the additional cash in bonds.

holdings are rather small in relation to turnover, it requires a rather large increase in the short-term rate of interest to effect any further curtailment of cash holdings. Thus, at such a point a rather large increase in the short-term rate of interest is

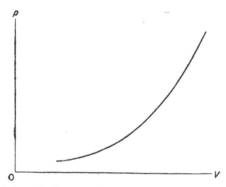

FIG. 3. Relationship between the velocity of circulation, V, and the short-term rate of interest, ρ.

required to effect a given increment in the velocity of circulation, ΔV. On the other hand, when cash is very plentiful in relation to turnover, economies in cash are easily achievable and the rise in the rate of interest required to make possible an increase in the velocity of circulation, ΔV, is small.

Statistical illustration

We shall apply the above to an analysis of changes in the short-term rate of interest in the United Kingdom in the period 1930–1938. For this period figures of turnover (debit entries to current accounts) of the London Clearing Banks are available. Although the ratio of these to the level of current accounts appears at first sight to give us the velocity of circulation, unfortunately the case is not so simple.

The turnover consists of two parts of very different character: financial and non-financial transactions. For 1930 financial transactions were estimated to constitute about 85 per cent[1] of the total turnover. On the other hand, financial current accounts are unlikely to be more than one-third of the total.[2] This dis-

[1] E. H. Phelps Brown and G. L. S. Shackle, *Statistics of Monetary Circulation in England and Wales*, 1919–1937 (Royal Economic Society, Memorandum No. 74), p. 28.　　　　　　　　　　　　　　　[2] *Ibid.*, p. 3.

proportion obviously reflects the much greater velocity of circulation of financial, compared with non-financial, accounts. As a result, a change in the proportion of financial to non-financial accounts will cause a considerable change in the ratio of turnover to current accounts even though both velocities of circulation remain unaltered. This defect can be remedied in the following way. We reduce the weight of financial transactions by multiplying them by that factor which brings the ratio of financial to non-financial transactions in the base year 1930 to the level of the ratio of financial to non-financial current accounts in that year. Next we add the 'reduced financial transactions' to the non-financial transactions and divide the sum by total current accounts. This ratio may be considered an approximate index of changes in the velocity of circulation. This calculation is described in detail in my paper on 'The Short-term Rate of Interest and the Velocity of Circulation.'[1] The results obtained there are given in Table 16 and plotted in Fig. 4.[2]

Table 16. Index of Velocity of Circulation and the Short-Term Rate of Interest in the United Kingdom, 1930–1938

Year	Velocity of Circulation (1930 = 100)	Rate on Treasury Bills (in percentages)
1930	100	2·48
1931	95	3·59
1932	93	1·49
1933	83	0·59
1934	88	0·73
1935	85	0·55
1936	82	0·58
1937	84	0·56
1938	80	0·61

Source: Bank of England, Statistical Summary.

As may be seen, except for 1931, the points of relationship of ρ and V lie around a curve of the shape which we deduced on *a priori* grounds in the preceding section. 1931 is considerably above the curve. This is explained by the financial crisis in the second half of that year which caused an upward

[1] *Review of Economic Statistics*, May 1941.
[2] The results are slightly revised, allowance having been made for: (1) a change in the working practice of Town Clearings in November 1932, which increased the volume of total clearings by about 2 per cent; (2) a change in the scope of current accounts in January 1938, which caused an increase of about 2 per cent.

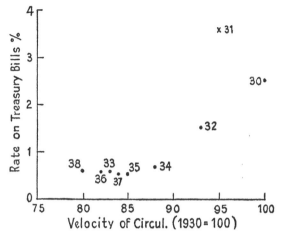

FIG. 4. Velocity of circulation and rate on Treasury Bills, United Kingdom, 1930–1938.

shift of the curve, i.e. increased the amount of cash required for a given turnover at a given short-term rate of interest.[1]

An analysis of the relationship between the short-term rate of interest and the velocity of circulation of cash balances of large manufacturing companies in the United States for the period 1919–1940 was carried out on the same lines by Mr. I. N. Behrman.[2] He arrives at similar results.

Changes in the supply of cash by banks

It follows from equation (11) that

$$MV(\rho) = T$$

In this form the equation is actually the quantity of money equation.[3] Its significance here, however, is quite different from that in the quantity theory of money. It shows that with a given value of transactions, T, an increase in the supply of money, M, by the banking system causes a fall in the short-term rate of interest.

The process by which banks increase the supply of money deserves to be considered in some detail. For the sake of

[1] The point for the year 1938 is also slightly raised by the increase of the short-term rate in the autumn, due to political events.

[2] 'The Short-Term Interest Rate and the Velocity of Circulation,' *Econometrica*, April 1948.

[3] T is the aggregate *value* of transactions and thus stands for PT in the Fisher equation.

simplicity let us assume that bank deposits consist only of current accounts. Imagine that banks decide to reduce their cash ratio (i.e. the ratio of the amount of notes and accounts in the Central Bank to deposits) and buy bills. The price of bills will rise and thus the short-term rate of interest will fall to that level at which the 'public' will be prepared to add to their current accounts the amount which the banks expend on bills.

It is of interest to note that the buying of bonds by banks will have similar repercussions. It is true that initially the price of bonds will rise and the yield of bonds will fall to a level which will induce the 'public' to shift from long-term assets to short-term assets and cash. But there will also be a tendency on the part of the 'public' to invest the additional cash received from the sale of bonds to the banks in bills; thus the price of bills will rise and the short-term rate will fall to the level at which the 'public' will be prepared to hold the additional cash rather than invest it in bills.

Cyclical changes in the short-term rate of interest

According to the above, cyclical fluctuations in the short-term rate of interest can be explained in terms of the supply

Table 17.   Short-Term Rate of Interest in the United Kingdom and the United States, 1929–1940

Year	Rate on Treasury Bills in the United Kingdom	Rate on prime commercial papers of 4 to 6 months in the United States
	(in percentages)	
1929	5·26	5·86
1930	2·48	3·59
1931	3·59	2·63
1932	1·49	2·73
1933	0·59	1·72
1934	0·73	1·02
1935	0·55	0·76
1936	0·58	0·75
1937	0·56	0·95
1938	0·61	0·81
1939	*	0·59
1940	*	0·56

(*) War years.

Source: Bank of England, Statistical Summary; Board of Governors of the Federal Reserve System, Banking and Monetary Statistics.

of cash by banks in response to fluctuations in the value of transactions, T. It appears that in general this supply of cash fluctuates less than the value of transactions so that the velocity of circulation and the short-term rate of interest increase in the boom and fall in the slump.

It should be added that the movements of the short-term rate of interest in the 'thirties both in the United Kingdom and in the United States are not quite typical in pattern.

Both in the United Kingdom and in the United States there is a sharp fall in the depression years (with a temporary reversal in 1931 in the United Kingdom and in 1932 in the United States reflecting the financial panic). However, in the years of recovery the short-term rate continues to fall, thus reflecting a basic shift towards 'easy money' in banking policy.

7

The Long-Term Rate of Interest

The short-term rate and the long-term rate

It has been shown in the preceding chapter that the short-term rate of interest is determined by the volume of transactions and the supply of cash by the banking system. We shall now examine the problem of the determination of the long-term rate of interest.

In order to establish a connection between the short-term and the long-term rate of interest, we shall examine the problem of substitution between a representative short-term asset, say a bill of exchange, and a representative long-term asset, say a Consol. Imagine a person or enterprise considering how to invest its reserves. The security holder is likely to compare the results of holding various types of securities for a few years. Thus, in comparing the yields he takes into account the expected average discount rate over this period, which we denote by ρ_e, and the present long-term rate of interest (yield of Consols), r. We may now examine the advantages and disadvantages of both types of securities, the net result of which accounts for the difference $r - \rho_e$.

We may first consider the possibility of a capital loss. The holding of bills guarantees the integrity of the principal. On the other hand, bonds may depreciate in value during the period considered. Short-period fluctuations in the value of securities owned may be disregarded by the holder, but if the capital loss proves to have a more permanent character, it must be accounted as such.[1] Therefore, a provision for the

---

[1] It should be noticed that the loss is due to depreciation of the bond *per se* and not to the need of converting it into cash at a time when the market position is unfavourable. The cash required in an emergency can always be obtained by means of bank credit granted on the security of the bonds up to a high percentage of their value.

risk of depreciation in value, γ, must be taken into account when the yields r and ρ_e are compared.

On the other hand, there are certain advantages involved in holding bonds as compared with bills. The expected rate of discount, ρ_e, is subject to uncertainty while the rate of interest on bonds, r, is not. Moreover, the holding of bills which must be re-bought every three months involves various inconveniences and costs. These considerations, however, are not very important and the advantages, ϵ, of bond holding from this point of view are not apt to be valued at more than, say, 1 per cent.

If we consider the net effect of the disadvantages, γ, and the advantages, ϵ, of holding a bond we have:

$$r - \rho_e = \gamma - \epsilon \qquad (12)$$

We may give further consideration to the value of γ. If the present price of Consols is p and the holder has a certain, more or less definite, idea based on past experience about the minimum to which this price may fall, p_{min}, it is plausible to assume that γ is roughly proportionate to $\dfrac{p - p_{min}}{p}$, i.e. to the maximum percentage by which the price of Consols is considered apt to fall. We thus have

$$\gamma = g\frac{p - p_{min}}{p} = g\left(1 - \frac{p_{min}}{p}\right) \qquad (13)$$

If the period for which the calculation is made were one year and the depreciation in capital value were considered certain, g would be equal to 100. But since the period is normally longer and the maximum depreciation not very probable, g may be expected to be much less than one hundred.

As the price of Consols is in inverse proportion to their yield, expression (13) may be written:

$$\gamma = g\left(1 - \frac{r}{r_{max}}\right) \qquad (13')$$

where r_{max} is the yield corresponding to the 'minimum price,' p_{min}. By substituting this expression for γ in equation (12) we obtain, after simple transformations:

$$r = \frac{\rho_e}{1 + \dfrac{g}{r_{max}}} + \frac{g - \epsilon}{1 + \dfrac{g}{r_{max}}} \qquad (14)$$

If the coefficients g, ϵ and r_{max} are stable, this equation expresses the long-term rate, r, as a linear function of the expected short-term rate, ρ_e. It may be seen that (g, ϵ, and r_{max} being stable) r always changes by a smaller amount than ρ_e, since $1 + \dfrac{g}{r_{max}} > 1$. This follows from our assumption that when r increases the risk of the depreciation of Consols declines (equation 13′).

We have thus two factors explaining the stability of the long-term rate as compared with the short-term rate of interest. (1) The short-run changes in the short-term rate, ρ, are only partly reflected in the estimates of ρ_e. (2) The long-term rate, r, changes by a smaller amount than ρ_e, the average short-term rate expected over the next few years.

It is important to note that the 'risk coefficient' may increase not only when the depreciation of bonds is considered more likely, but also when the proportion of holdings of long-term assets to holdings of short-term assets plus cash rises. For then, with the same probability of depreciation in bond values, an actual fall means a greater loss relative to the value of all liquid assets. This 'increasing risk' is accounted for by a higher g. Thus, *ceteris paribus*, if the amount of long-term assets relative to all liquid assets held by the public rises, g tends to increase.

Moreover, the coefficient g also depends on the rate of income taxes (from which we have so far abstracted). Indeed, the difference between the long-term yield and the short-term yield is subject to tax, but depreciation in the value of bonds is not usually accounted in making the tax assessment or at least not fully accounted. This introduces an additional disadvantage in the holding of bonds as compared with bills, and thus the coefficient g is correspondingly higher.

Application to the yields of British Consols. 1849–1938

We shall now apply the results arrived at in the last section to the analysis of yields of Consols in the period 1849–1938. A time curve of the yield of Consols is presented in Fig. 5. It will be seen that it is possible to sub-divide this period into ten very unequal intervals, within each of which the long-term rate undergoes relatively small fluctuations round the average as compared with the changes between the intervals: 1949–1880, 1881–1887, 1888–1893, 1894–1900, 1901–1909, 1910–1914, 1915–1918, 1919–1921, 1922–1931, 1932–1938. This may be

82

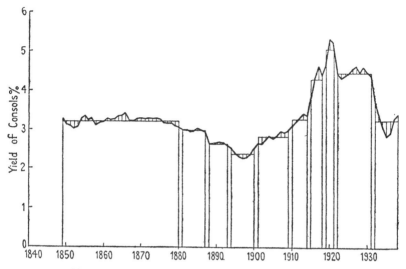

FIG. 5. Yield of Consols, United Kingdom, 1849–1938.

accounted for by an hypothesis that within each of these intervals the expected short-term rate ρ_e and the coefficients g, r_{max} and ϵ fluctuated rather little around certain values while they underwent more basic changes from interval to interval.

Let us turn our attention to these changes in the expected average discount rate ρ_e. Within each of our intervals the discount rate ρ in fact underwent distinct fluctuations which did not, however, cause important fluctuations in ρ_e. This may be accounted for by the following hypothesis: the investors in their estimates of ρ_e disregarded to a great extent the 'high' and 'low' levels of the discount rate within the intervals, classifying them as temporary, and based their expectations chiefly on the most recent 'medium' position; and the spread of these 'medium values' was rather small within each period. If this hypothesis is correct, it follows that the average ρ_e in each period does not differ much from the average of the actual rate of discount ρ in that period. On this assumption we may take the average discount rate in each period to be our first approximation of the average ρ_e and thus may correlate the average yields of Consols and average discount rates within the selected periods and analyse the regression equations by means of formula (14).

83

The average yield of Consols and the average discount rate for the selected periods from 1849 to 1938 are given in Table 18.

Table 18. The Average Yield of Consols and the Average Discount Rate, Selected Periods, 1849–1938

Interval	Average yield of Consols	Average Discount Rate
	(in percentages)	
1849–1880	3·21	3·66
1881–1887	2·98	2·82
1888–1893	2·63	2·68
1894–1900	2·38	2·18
1901–1909	2·82	3·09
1910–1914	3·27	3·4
1915–1918	4·30	4·3
1919–1921	5·07	5·09
1922–1931	4·48	3·76
1932–1938	3·25	0·82

Source: T. T. Williams, 'The Rate of Discount and the Price of Consols,' Journal of the Royal Statistical Society, *February* 1912; *United Kingdom, Annual Abstract of Statistics; Bank of England,* Statistical Summary.

Fig. 6 presents the same data on a scatter diagram. It will be seen that most of the points lie very close to two straight lines AB and A_1B_1. The points corresponding to the intervals before World War I lie close to the line AB except those representing 1881–1887 and 1910–1914. The points corresponding to the post-war periods lie close to the line A_1B_1, which is considerably above AB. Finally, the war period 1915–1918 is represented by a point lying between AB and A_1B_1. It must be noticed that the position of the point 1881–1887 above AB is accounted for by the fact that the yield of Consols in this period did not reflect the level of the 'pure long-term rate' but was 'too high' owing to expected conversion.[1]

The results obtained may be plausibly interpreted in terms of formula (14). In the period 1849–1909 the coefficients g, r_{max} and ϵ were more or less stable, and therefore we have a linear functional relationship between r and ρ_e represented by AB. After this period these coefficients underwent a definite change, chiefly during World War I, and then became stable again in the post-war period, so that the points ρ_e and r are in this period situated on the straight line A_1B_1. The points 1910–

[1] See R. G. Hawtrey, *A Century of Bank Rate*, London, 1938.

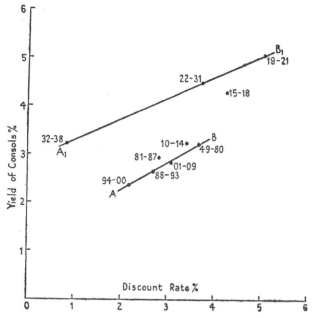

FIG. 6. Discount rate and yield of Consols, United Kingdom, 1849–1938.

1914 and 1915–1918, lying between AB and A_1B_1, represent the period during which the shift from AB to A_1B_1 occurred.

From the equations of the lines AB and A_1B_1 the coefficients g and ϵ may now be obtained for the 1849–1909 and 1919–1938 periods respectively.

The equation of AB (1849–1909) is

$$r = 0 \cdot 550\, \rho_e + 1 \cdot 17$$

If we compare it with formula (14),

$$r = \frac{\rho_e}{1 + \dfrac{g}{r_{max}}} + \frac{g - \epsilon}{1 + \dfrac{g}{r_{max}}} \tag{14}$$

we obtain two equations

$$\frac{1}{1 + \dfrac{g}{r_{max}}} = 0 \cdot 550 \quad \text{and} \quad \frac{g - \epsilon}{1 + \dfrac{g}{r_{max}}} = 1 \cdot 17$$

With regard to the expected maximum long-term rate we may assume that it is approximately $3 \cdot 4$, for this was the maximum

85

rate in the period in question and the level of r at the beginning of the period was not much lower. It is then possible to determine from the last equations the coefficients g and ϵ. We obtain: $g = 2 \cdot 78$, $\epsilon = 0 \cdot 65$.

The equation for the period 1919–1938 is

$$r = 0 \cdot 425 \, \rho_e + 2 \cdot 90$$

and consequently

$$\frac{1}{1 + \dfrac{g}{r_{max}}} = 0 \cdot 425 \quad \text{and} \quad \frac{g - \epsilon}{1 + \dfrac{g}{r_{max}}} = 2 \cdot 90$$

Here r_{max} may be assumed equal to $5 \cdot 1$, this being the level reached at the beginning of the period and never exceeded thereafter. Thus, we obtain: $g = 6 \cdot 9$, $\epsilon = 0 \cdot 07$.

We may now put together the results of our calculation:

Period	g	r_{max}	ϵ
1849–1909	2·78	3·40	0·65
1919–1938	6·90	5·10	0·07

From the point of view of confirming our theory the most important result is that ϵ (the advantage, abstracting from the risk of depreciation, of bonds as compared with bills) is small, as we expected it to be for *a priori* reasons. If the coefficient of ρ_e in the post-war period had been not $0 \cdot 425$ but, say, $0 \cdot 25$, we should, *ceteris paribus*, have obtained for ϵ the value $3 \cdot 7$, which would be obviously absurd and so would disprove our theory.[1]

The coefficient g is small as compared with 100, both in the pre-war and the post-war periods—which is again in accordance with *a priori* argument. The considerable rise in g (about $2 \cdot 5$ times) between these two periods is explained by the much greater fluctuations in r after 1914 and by the rise in income taxes and surtaxes. The definite rise in g in combination with the increase in r_{max} accounts for the shift of the line AB to the position A_1B_1.

[1] The theory would not be disproved, however, if ϵ were small and negative, although according to our theory it should be positive. The empirical inquiry outlined here is of necessity approximate in character and thus may easily render a small negative ϵ instead of a small positive one.

Stability of the long-term rate of interest during the business cycle

A glance at Fig. 5 will show that major changes in the long-term rate do not follow a six- to ten-year cyclical pattern. Apart from minor fluctuations there is something like one wave from 1849 to 1914. This period is followed by that of the war and post-war inflation. After the descent from the peak reached at the beginning of the twenties the long-term rate is stabilized until the Great Depression when a downward trend continuing into the second half of the 'thirties appears. The reversal of this trend in the last two years before World War II is due to the political situation.

In Table 19 the yield on Consols is given for the period 1929–1938 and the yield of U.S. treasury bonds for 1929–1940.

Table 19. The Long-Term Rate of Interest in the United Kingdom and the United States during the Great Depression

Year	Yield on U.K. 2½% Consols	Yield on U.S. Treasury Bonds
	(in percentages)	
1929	4·60	3·60
1930	4·48	3·29
1931	4·39	3·34
1932	3·74	3·68
1933	3·39	3·31
1934	3·10	3·12
1935	2·89	2·79
1936	2·94	2·69
1937	3·27	2·74
1938	3·37	2·61
1939	*	2·41
1940	*	2·26

(*) War years.

Source: Bank of England Statistical Summary; *Board of Governors of the Federal Reserve System*, Banking and Monetary Statistics.

In both countries the main feature is the downward trend which results from the long-run fall in the short-term rate. However, the American series differs at two points: (*a*) there is a significant increase in the United States long-term rate in 1932 reflecting the intensity of the financial panic; (*b*) there is no rise in 1937 and 1938 in contrast to the United Kingdom where the long-term rate was affected by the world political situation. In neither series can any definite cyclical pattern be seen. In particular, there is no significant fall like that in the short-term rate until 1934.

The fact that the long-term rate does not show marked cyclical fluctuations is fully in line with the above theory. The short-term rate normally falls in a slump and rises in a boom because the supply of money undergoes smaller fluctuations than the value of transactions. But the long-term rate reflects these fluctuations only to a small extent. Indeed, the long-term rate is based on the average short-term rate expected in the next few years rather than on the current short-term rate; moreover, the long-term rate changes considerably less than the expected short-term rate because the increase in it, that is, the fall in the price of bonds, makes the risk of their further depreciation less likely (see p. 82).

Some authors have attributed to the rate of interest an important role among the forces underlying economic fluctuations. As it is the long-term rate that is relevant to the determination of investment and thus to the mechanism of the cyclical process, the results arrived at above are of considerable significance. Indeed, in view of the fact that the long-term rate of interest, for reasons discussed above, does not show marked cyclical fluctuations, it can hardly be considered an important element in the mechanism of the business cycle.[1]

[1] Cf. p. 99 below.

Part 4

Determination of Investment

8

Entrepreneurial Capital and Investment

The size of the firm and entrepreneurial capital

Two factors are usually mentioned as limiting the size of a firm: (1) dis-economies of a large scale; and (2) limitations of market, the expansion of which would require unprofitable price reductions or increases in selling costs. The first of these factors seems to be rather unrealistic. It has no technological basis because, although every plant has an optimum size, it is still possible to have two, three, or more plants. The argument with respect to difficulties of management arising out of large-scale enterprise also seems doubtful since adequate measures of decentralization can always be introduced to meet this problem. The limitation of the size of the firm by the market for its products is real enough but it leaves unexplained the existence of large and small firms in the same industry.

There is, however, another factor which is of decisive importance in limiting the size of a firm: the amount of the entrepreneurial capital, i.e. the amount of capital owned by the firm. The access of a firm to the capital market, or in other words the amount of rentier capital it may hope to obtain, is determined to a large extent by the amount of its entrepreneurial capital. It would be impossible for a firm to borrow capital above a certain level determined by the amount of its entrepreneurial capital. If, for instance, a firm should attempt to float a bond issue which was too large in terms of its entrepreneurial capital, this issue would not be subscribed in full. Even if the firm should undertake to issue the bonds at a higher rate of interest than that prevailing, the sale of bonds might not be improved since the higher rate in itself might raise misgivings with regard to the future solvency of the firm.

In addition, many firms will not use to the full the potentialities of the capital market because of the 'increasing risk' involved in expansion. Indeed, some firms may even keep their investment at a level below that of the entreprenuerial capital, a part of which may be held in securities. A firm considering expansion must face the fact that, given the amount of the entrepreneurial capital, the risk increases with the amount invested. The greater the investment in relation to the entrepreneurial capital, the greater is the reduction of the entrepreneur's income in the event of an unsuccessful business venture. Suppose, for instance, that an entrepreneur fails to make any return on his business. Now, if only a part of his capital is invested in business and a part is held in first-rate bonds, he will still derive some net income from his capital. If all of his capital is invested his income will be zero, while, if he has borrowed, he will suffer a net loss which, if it continues long enough, must drive his business out of existence. It is clear that the heavier the borrowing the greater will be the danger of such a contingency.

The size of a firm thus appears to be circumscribed by the amount of its entrepreneurial capital both through its influence on the capacity to borrow capital and through its effect on the degree of risk. The variety in the size of enterprises in the same industry at a given time can be easily explained in terms of differences in entrepreneurial capital. A firm with a large entreprenuerial capital could obtain funds for a large investment whereas a firm with a small entrepreneurial capital could not. Differences in the position of firms arising out of differences in their entrepreneurial capital are further enhanced by the fact that firms below a certain size have no access whatever to the capital market.

It follows from the above that the expansion of the firm depends on its accumulation of capital out of current profits. This will enable the firm to undertake new investment without encountering the obstacles of the limited capital market or 'increasing risk.' Not only can savings out of current profits be directly invested in the business, but this increase in the firm's capital will make it possible to contract new loans.

The problem of joint-stock companies

Legitimate doubt may arise as to whether the above limitations to investment are applicable in the case of joint-stock companies. If a company issues bonds or debentures the situation is not materially altered. The greater the issue the more are dividends impaired in the event of an unsuccessful business venture. The position is similar in the case of an issue of preference shares (the fixed return on which is paid from profit before any return accrues to ordinary shares). But what about an issue of ordinary shares? Prima facie it would seem that no limits are set to such an issue, but in fact there are quite a few restraining factors.

(*a*) It should first be stated that a joint-stock company is not a 'brotherhood of shareholders' but is managed by a controlling group of big shareholders while the rest of the shareholders do not differ from holders of bonds with a flexible rate of interest. Now, this group, if it is to continue to exercise control, cannot sell an unlimited number of shares to the 'public.' It is true that this 'difficulty' may be partly overcome, for instance, by building up holding companies.[1] Nevertheless, the problem of the maintenance of control by top shareholders exerts *some* restraining influence upon issues to the 'public.'

(*b*) There is a risk that the investment financed by an issue of shares may not increase company profits proportionately as much as the issue increased the share and reserve capital. If the rate of return on the new investment does not at least equal the old rate of profits, then the dividends of the old shareholders in general and of the controlling group in particular will be 'squeezed.' Risk of this type is, of course, the greater the larger the new issue. This is, therefore, another case of 'increasing risk.'

(*c*) Share issues are restrained by the limited market for shares of a given company. The 'public' tend to distribute their risks by holding a variety of shares. It will be impossible, therefore, to place more than a limited amount of new shares at a price which would be reasonable from the point of view

---

[1] A group possessing 51 per cent of shares of a company starts a new company to hold their shares. The group retains 51 per cent of the shares of the new company and sells 49 per cent to the public. It now controls the holding company and through it the old company with only about 26 per cent of the capital of the latter, while it has about 25 per cent of this capital in cash which it is free to invest in a new share issue of the old company.

of the old shareholders. For the latter the price at which new shares are sold is of crucial importance. Indeed, if this price is 'too low' in relation to expected profits, a situation similar to that considered under (b) will arise. The new issue will not increase the earning capacity of the company proportionately as much as its share and reserve capital and this will result in a 'squeezing' of the dividends of the old shareholders.

All this points to the fact that a joint-stock company also has definite limitations to its expansion. This expansion depends, as in the case of a family concern, on the accumulation of capital out of current profits. This increase in the entrepreneurial capital, however, is not confined to the undistributed profits of the company. Subscriptions of share issues by the controlling group which are closely connected with the group's 'personal' savings should be considered as another form of accumulation of entrepreneurial capital.

The 'internal' accumulation of capital provides resources which can be 'ploughed back' into the business. Moreover, such an accumulation facilitates new issues of shares to the 'public' because it helps to overcome the obstacles enumerated above. (a) When the accumulation takes the form of subscriptions to share issues by the controlling group, it permits the issue of a certain amount of shares to the 'public' without infringing upon the command of the group over the majority of shares. (b) A growth in the size of the firm through 'internal accumulation of capital decreases the risk involved in issuing a given amount of shares to the 'public' to finance new investment. (c) An increase in the capital of the company without recourse to the 'public' will tend to widen the capital market for the shares of that company since, in general, the larger a company is the more important will its role in the share market be.

Concluding remarks

The limitation of the size of the firm by the availability of entrepreneurial capital goes to the very heart of the capitalist system. Many economists assume, at least in their abstract theories, a state of business democracy where anybody endowed with entrepreneurial ability can obtain capital for starting a business venture. This picture of the activities of the 'pure' entrepreneur is, to put it mildly, unrealistic. The most important prerequisite for becoming an entrepreneur is the *ownership* of capital.

The above considerations are of great importance for the theory of determination of investment. One of the important factors of investment decisions is the accumulation of firms' capital out of current profits. We shall deal with this subject in detail in the next chapter.[1]

[1] The problems discussed here are also of considerable importance for the theory of concentration of capital: cf. J. Steindl, 'Capitalist Enterprise and Risk,' *Oxford Economic Papers*, March 1945.

9

Determinants of Investment

Determinants of fixed capital investment decisions

Our problem here is to find the determinants of the *rate* of investment decisions, i.e. the amount of investment decisions *per unit of time*. Investment decisions in a given period, determined by certain factors operating in that period, are followed by actual investment with a time lag. The time lag is largely due to the period of construction, but also reflects such factors as delayed entrepreneurial reactions. If the amount of fixed capital investment decisions per unit of time is denoted by D, and investment in fixed capital by F, we shall have the relation:

$$F_{t+\tau} = D_t \tag{15}$$

where the lag, τ, is the horizontal distance between the time curve of investment decisions per unit of time, D, and the time curve of investment in fixed capital, F.[1]

We shall approach the problem of the determinants of fixed capital investment decisions as follows. If we consider the rate of investment decisions in a short period we can assume that at the beginning of this period the firms have pushed their investment plans up to a point where they cease to be profitable either because of the limited market for the firm's products or because of 'increasing risk' and limitation of the capital market. New investment decisions will thus be made only if in the period considered, changes in the economic situation take place which extend the boundaries set to investment plans by those factors. We shall take into consideration three broad categories of such changes in the given period: (*a*) gross

[1] It should be noticed that investment decisions are not strictly irrevocable. The cancellation of investment orders, although involving considerable loss, can and does take place. This is a factor, therefore, which disturbs the relationship between investment decisions and investment as described by equation (15).

96

accumulation of capital by firms out of current profits, i.e. their current gross savings; and (b) changes in profits and changes in the stock of fixed capital which determine conjointly changes in the rate of profit. Let us examine these factors in more detail.

The first factor has been dealt with in a general way in the preceding chapter. Investment decisions are closely related to 'internal' accumulation of capital, i.e. to the gross savings of firms. There will be a tendency to use these savings for invest-ment, and, in addition, investment may be financed by new outside funds on the strength of the accumulation of entre-preneurial capital. The gross savings of firms thus extend the boundaries set to investment plans by the limited capital market and the factor of 'increasing risk.'

The gross savings of firms consist, strictly speaking, of depreciation and undistributed profits. We shall include with these, however, the 'personal savings' of the controlling groups invested in their own companies through subscriptions to new share issues. This concept of gross savings of firms is thus somewhat vague. We shall get around this difficulty by assuming that the gross savings of firms as conceived above are related to total gross private savings (*inter alia* as a result of the corre-lation between profits and national income, see p. 59 above). On this assumption the rate of capital investment decisions, D, is an increasing function of total gross savings, S. (We imagine that investment decisions and investment are in real terms— i.e. their values are deflated by the index of prices of investment goods. Thus, it follows directly that gross savings also have to be deflated by the index of prices of investment goods.)

Another factor which influences the rate of investment decisions is the increase in profits per unit of time. A rise in profits from the beginning to the end of the period considered renders attractive certain projects which were previously con-sidered unprofitable and thus permits an extension of the boundaries of investment plans in the course of the period. The value of the resulting new investment decisions divided by the length of the period gives us the contribution of the change of profits per unit of time to the rate of investment decisions in the period considered.

When the profitability of new investment projects is being weighed, expected profits are considered in relation to the value of the new capital equipment. Thus, profits are taken in relation to the current prices of investment goods. We can allow for this factor by deflating profits by the price index of investment goods. In other words, if we shall denote aggregate gross profits after taxes deflated by the prices of investment goods by P,[1] we can say that *ceteris paribus* the rate of investment decisions, D, is an increasing function of $\frac{\Delta P}{\Delta t}$.

Finally, the net increment of capital equipment per unit of time affects adversely the rate of investment decisions, i.e. without this effect the rate of investment decisions would be higher. Indeed, an increase in the volume of capital equipment if profits, P, are constant means a reduction in the rate of profit. Just as an increase in profits within the period considered renders additional investment projects attractive, so an accumulation of capital equipment tends to restrict the boundaries of investment plans. This effect is most easily seen in the case where new enterprises enter the field and thereby render investment plans of the established firms less attractive. If we denote the value of the stock of capital equipment deflated by appropriate prices by K we can say that the rate of investment decisions, D, is *ceteris paribus* a decreasing function of $\frac{\Delta K}{\Delta t}$.

To sum up: the rate of investment decisions, D, is, as a first approximation, an increasing function of gross savings, S, and of the rate of change in aggregate profits, $\frac{\Delta P}{\Delta t}$, and a decreasing function of the rate of change in the stock of capital equipment, $\frac{\Delta K}{\Delta t}$. Assuming, moreover, a linear relation we have:

$$D = aS + b\frac{\Delta P}{\Delta t} - c\frac{\Delta K}{\Delta t} + d \qquad (16)$$

where d is a constant subject to long-run changes.
As according to equation (15):

$$F_{t+\tau} = D_t$$

---

[1] The concept of 'real' gross profits, P, in Chapters 3, 4 and 5 differs from the present one in that there the price index implicit in the deflation of the gross product of the private sector was used as deflator.

we also have for investment in fixed capital at time t:

$$F_{t+\tau} = aS_t + b\frac{\Delta P_t}{\Delta t} - c\frac{\Delta K_t}{\Delta t} + d \qquad (16')$$

Factors not taken into consideration

It may be questioned why changes in the rate of interest, which have an opposite effect to changes in profits, were not considered as a co-determinant of investment decisions. This simplification is based on the fact that according to the above (see p. 88) the long-term rate of interest (as measured by yields of government bonds) does not show marked cyclical fluctuations.

It is true that the yields of business debentures sometimes increase appreciably during depressions because of crises of confidence. The omission of this factor does not invalidate the above theory since the rise in the yields of the securities in question works in the same direction as the fall in profits (although it is of much less significance). Thus, this effect may be roughly accounted for in the discussion of the business cycle by a somewhat higher coefficient b in equation (16).

It is still necessary, however, to consider the problem raised by the fluctuations of share yields, that is, of the ratios of current dividends to share prices. The movement of yields of preference shares shows very much the same pattern as that of the yields of debentures and may be taken into consideration in the same way. This is not, however, at least not fully, the case for ordinary shares. Although this factor seems to be in general of limited importance this is not to deny that it may vitiate to some extent the application of the above theory.

We shall now consider briefly an entirely different factor which was not taken into account in building up equation (16), namely, innovations. We assume that innovations, in the sense of gradual adjustments of the equipment of a firm to the current state of technology, are part and parcel of 'ordinary' investment as determined by this formula. The immediate effect of a new invention is discussed in Chapter 15 in connection with the theory of economic development. It will be seen there that these effects are reflected in the level of d. The same is true of the long-run changes in the rate of interest or in the share yields.

Two special cases of the theory

It can be shown that equation (16) covers, as special cases, some of the existing theories of investment decisions.

Let us first assume that the coefficients a and c are equal to zero so that the equation is reduced to

$$D = b\frac{\Delta P}{\Delta t} + d$$

Let us assume in addition that d is equal to depreciation. It follows that net investment is determined by the rate of change in 'real' profits. This case corresponds roughly to the so-called acceleration principle. It is true that this principle establishes a relationship between net investment and the rate of change in output rather than in profits and that the theoretical foundations are different from those given above, but the final results are much the same because of the inter-relationship between 'real' profits and aggregate output (see Chapter 5).

With respect to the theoretical problem, it would appear to be more realistic to base the 'acceleration principle' on the grounds suggested above (see p. 97) than to deduce it, from the necessity of expanding capacity in order to increase output. It is well known that large reserve capacities exist, at least throughout a considerable part of the cycle, and that output, therefore, may increase without an actual increase in existing capacities. But, whatever the basis of the 'acceleration principle' may be, it is inadequate not only because it does not take into consideration the other determinants of investment decisions examined above, but also because it does not agree with the facts. In the course of the business cycle the highest rate of increase in output will be somewhere close to the medium position (see Fig. 7). It would follow from the 'acceleration principle' that the highest level of investment decisions would come into existence at that time. This, however, is unrealistic. Indeed, it would mean that the time lag between investment decisions and aggregate output would be about one-fourth of the business cycle or $1\cdot5$ to $2\cdot5$ years. As it is difficult to assume that the time lag between investment decisions and actual investment would be more than one year,[1] it would mean that the actual investment in fixed capital would 'lead' output by $0\cdot5$ to $1\cdot5$ years. The available data do not sub-

[1] Cf. p. 109 below.

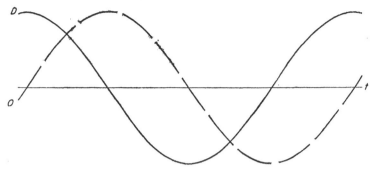

FIG. 7. Fixed capital investment decisions, *D*, and aggregate output, *O* (reduced to the same amplitude) according to the 'acceleration principle.'

stantiate such a lag. This will be seen, for instance, from Fig. 8 where the time curves of investment in fixed capital and output (gross product of the private sector) are given for the United States for the period 1929–1940.[1] It appears that no appreciable

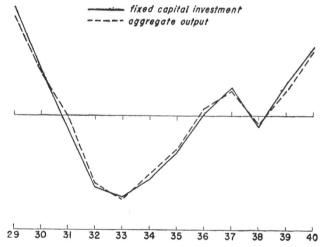

FIG. 8. Fluctuations in fixed capital investment and gross product of the private sector (reduced to the same amplitude and after the elimination of the intervening trend), United States, 1929–1940.

time lag is discernible. The regression equation, patterned on our equation (16'), which we obtain below for United States

[1] The time curves are reduced to the same amplitude and the intervening trend is eliminated. (For details see Statistical Appendix, Note 10.)

101

investment in fixed capital for this period (see p. 112), also does not conform at all to the 'acceleration principle.'

We obtain the second special case of our theory by assuming that a given amount of new savings affects investment decisions to an equal extent, that is, by assuming that a is equal to 1. We also assume that the constant d is equal to 0. Thus, we have:

$$D = S + b\frac{\Delta P}{\Delta t} - c\frac{\Delta K}{\Delta t}$$

If in addition the assumption is made that inventories are stable throughout the cycle and that the export surplus and the budget deficit are both equal to zero, it follows that savings, S, are equal to actual investment in fixed capital, F (because savings are equal to investment in fixed capital and inventories plus export surplus plus budget deficit). We thus obtain:

$$D = F + b\frac{\Delta P}{\Delta t} - c\frac{\Delta K}{\Delta t}$$

and taking into consideration that $F_t = D_{t-\tau}$

$$D_t = D_{t-\tau} + b\frac{\Delta P_t}{\Delta t} - c\frac{\Delta K_t}{\Delta t}$$

or $$D_t - D_{t-\tau} = b\frac{\Delta P_t}{\Delta t} - c\frac{\Delta K_t}{\Delta t}$$

Now it is clear from the last equation that if profits, P, and the stock of capital equipment, K, are constant, so is the rate of investment decisions, D (because $D_t = D_{t-\tau}$). When profits increase to a new level, so does D (because during the period when P is increasing $D_t > D_{t-\tau}$). When the stock of capital equipment, K, rises to a new level, D declines (because during the period when K is increasing $D_t < D_{t-\tau}$). It follows that the rate of investment decisions is an increasing function of the level of profits and a decreasing function of the stock of capital equipment. This is the relationship which was the basis of the theory of the business cycle given in my *Essays on the Theory of Economic Fluctuations*. Thus this theory also appears to be a special case of the present one.

It is sometimes assumed that the relationship obtained here as a special case is operative under all conditions, on the following grounds. The expected rate of profit may be assumed

102

to be an increasing function of 'real' current profits and a decreasing function of the stock of capital equipment. It is further considered obvious that the higher the expected rate of profits the higher the level of investment in fixed capital will be.[1] The latter, however, is plausible only at first glance. The relation ceases to be obvious when it is remembered that we consider here the amount of investment decisions *per unit of time*. If a certain level of the rate of profits is maintained for some time, then the firm would make all the investment decisions which correspond to that rate of profits so that after that, unless some new facts came into the picture, no decisions would be forthcoming. It is the full reinvestment of savings coupled with the equality of savings and investment in fixed capital that assures, in the special case considered, the maintenance of the level of investment decisions per unit of time when the rate of profits is constant. But once these fairly rigid assumptions are dropped the theorem ceases to be true and a more general approach based on the equation $D = aS + b\dfrac{\Delta P}{\Delta t} - c\dfrac{\Delta K}{\Delta t} + d$ is necessary.

Examination of the fundamental equation

Before proceeding with an examination of the coefficients of equation (16′) it will be useful to alter it somewhat. Let us first take into consideration the fact that the rate of change in fixed capital equipment is equal to investment in fixed capital net of depreciation in the same period:

$$\frac{\Delta K}{\Delta t} = F - \delta$$

where δ is depreciation of equipment due to wear and tear and obsolescence. Thus, equation (16′) can be written as follows:

$$F_{t+\tau} = aS_t + b\frac{\Delta P_t}{\Delta t} - c(F_t - \delta) + d$$

Let us now transfer $- cF_t$ from the right-hand to the left-hand side of the equation and divide both sides of the equation by $1 + c$:

$$\frac{F_{t+\tau} + cF_t}{1 + c} = \frac{a}{1 + c}S_t + \frac{b}{1 + c}\frac{\Delta P_t}{\Delta t} + \frac{c\delta + d}{1 + c}$$

[1] Such was also my conception in my early papers in *Revue d'Economie Politique* and *Econometrica* referred to above.

The left-hand side of the equation is then a weighted average of $F_{t+\tau}$ and F_t. We can assume as a good approximation that it is equal to an intermediate value $F_{t+\theta}$ where θ is a time lag less than τ. As c is likely to be a rather small fraction,[1] θ is of the same order as τ. We can now write:

$$F_{t+\theta} = \frac{a}{1+c}S_t + \frac{b}{1+c}\frac{\Delta P_t}{\Delta t} + \frac{c\delta + d}{1+c}$$

The determinants of investment in fixed capital are thus reduced to past savings and to the past rate of change in profits. The negative effect of an increase in the stock of capital equipment is reflected in the denominator $1 + c$. To simplify the form of the equation we shall denote

$$\frac{b}{1+c} = b' \text{ and } \frac{c\delta + d}{1+c} = d'$$

No such abbreviation will, however, be introduced for $\dfrac{a}{1+c}$ because its dependence on a and c (the coefficients of savings, S, and of the rate of change in the stock of capital equipment, $\dfrac{\Delta K}{\Delta t}$, respectively, in the initial equation) is of significance for the subsequent discussion. We thus can write our equation finally in the form

$$F_{t+\theta} = \frac{a}{1+c}S_t + b'\frac{\Delta P_t}{\Delta t} + d' \tag{17}$$

We shall now examine the coefficients of this equation. The constant d' is subject to long-run changes.[2] An analysis of the

[1] Cyclical fluctuations in the stock of capital, K, in percentage terms are rather small. Thus, changes in the rate of profit resulting from this factor are small as well. Consequently, fluctuations in investment in fixed capital are accounted for to a much greater extent by changes in S and $\dfrac{\Delta P}{\Delta t}$ than by those in $\dfrac{\Delta K}{\Delta t}$ (although the latter may be of considerable significance in certain phases of the cycle, as will be seen in Chapter 11). In other words, the amplitude of fluctuations in $c\dfrac{\Delta K}{\Delta t}$ is much smaller than that in F. But as $\dfrac{\Delta K}{\Delta t}$ is the net investment in fixed capital (and the depreciation δ undergoes only slight cyclical fluctuations) this means that c is small as compared with 1.

[2] d' denotes $\dfrac{c\delta + d}{1+c}$. On p. 98 d was assumed to be a constant subject to long-run changes. Depreciation, δ, fluctuates only very little in the course of the business cycle, but in the long run it varies in line with the volume of capital equipment.

factors on which these changes depend is given in Chapter 15. However, as will be seen below its value is not relevant in a discussion of the business cycle. Nothing can be said on *a priori* basis about the coefficient b', although, as will be seen, its value is of decisive importance in determining the character of cyclical fluctuations. It will thus be necessary to consider a few alternative cases with different values of this coefficient. The only coefficient about which we shall make definite assumptions at this stage is $\dfrac{a}{1 + c}$.

The coefficient a, which indicates by how much investment decisions, D, increase as a result of increments in total current savings, S, will be influenced by various factors. First, the increment in the 'internal' savings of the firms which is relevant for investment decisions is smaller than the increment in total saving. This factor in itself would tend to make a less than 1. Another factor works in the same direction. The reinvestment of savings on a *ceteris paribus* basis, that is with constant aggregate profits, may encounter difficulties because the market for the firm's products is limited, and expansion into new spheres of activity involves considerable risk. On the other hand, an increment in 'internal' savings enables the firm to absorb outside funds at a higher rate if investment *is* considered desirable. This factor tends to increase investment decisions by more than the increment in 'internal' savings. These conflicting factors leave us still uncertain about whether a will be greater or less than 1.

The coefficient $\dfrac{a}{1 + c}$ is smaller than a because c is positive. According to the above, this reflects the negative influence upon investment decisions of an increasing stock of capital equipment. We shall assume that this coefficient is less than 1 for the following reasons. It will be seen below that with $\dfrac{a}{1 + c} \geqslant 1$ there would be in fact no business cycle at all (see Chapter 11), and the long-run development of the capitalist economy also would be different from the process we know (see Chapter 14). Moreover, the analysis of the United States data for the period 1929–1940 yields for $\dfrac{a}{1 + c}$ a value significantly less than 1.

Since the coefficient c is a rather small fraction (see p. 104 above) $\dfrac{a}{1+c} < 1$ means that a cannot be much higher than 1 (and, of course, it can be $\leqslant 1$).

Investment in inventories

In our analysis of investment in fixed capital we arrived at equation (17) which indicates that fixed capital investment decisions are a function both of the level of economic activity and of the rate of change in this level. Indeed, the amount of savings, S, in the equation is associated with the *level* of economic activity, while the rate of increase in profits, $\dfrac{\Delta P}{\Delta t}$, is related to the *rate of change* in this level. It is for this reason that the 'acceleration principle' which bases itself on the rate of change only is inadequate for the explanation of investment in fixed capital. However, for investment in inventories, the 'acceleration principle' seems to be a reasonable assumption.

It is indeed plausible to assume that the rate of change in the volume of inventories is roughly proportionate to the rate of change in output or the volume of sales. However, empirical investigations of changes in inventories show that here also a significant time lag between cause and effect is clearly discernible. This is accounted for by the fact that a rise in output and sales does not create any immediate need for an increase in inventories because a part of inventories serves as a reserve and, therefore, it is temporarily possible to increase the velocity of turnover of total inventories. It is only after some time that inventories are adjusted to the new higher level of output. Similarly, when output falls the volume of inventories is accordingly curtailed, but only after a certain delay and in the meantime there is a decline in their velocity of turnover.

There arises the question whether the availability of capital does not play a significant role in investment in inventories as it does in investment in fixed capital. In other words, whether we should not assume that investment in inventories depends not only on the rate of change in output, but on the influx of new savings as well. This, however, does not seem in general to be the case since inventories are semi-liquid assets and short-term credit can be depended upon to finance any expansion in step with output and sales.

In the light of the above we can relate investment in inventories, J, to the rate of change in output of the private sector, $\dfrac{\Delta O}{\Delta t}$, with a certain time lag. According to the information available this time lag seems to be of a similar order to that involved in fixed capital investment, τ. For the sake of simplicity we shall assume that the inventory time lag is equal to θ which is of the same order as τ. (See p. 104.) We thus can write for investment in inventories:

$$J_{t+\theta} = e\frac{\Delta O_t}{\Delta t} \qquad (18)$$

It should be noticed that the coefficient e and the time lag θ are really averages. The relationship between changes in inventories and changes in output is very different for various commodities, and changes in inventories have no direct relation to changes in output of services (also included in O_t). If any stability in e can be expected at all it is only on the basis of a correlation between fluctuations of various components of the total output of the private sector, O.

It should be noticed that the phenomenon of accumulation of unsold goods is accounted for at least partly by the time lag θ in the equation (18). Indeed, when the volume of sales stops rising and begins to fall, inventories according to our formula will continue to rise for a time. This is not to deny, however, that in such circumstances the accumulation of unsold goods may continue on a larger scale than suggested by this formula. This deviation from the formula probably does not have a very serious bearing upon the overall theory of the trade cycle because this 'abnormal' accumulation of inventories is frequently liquidated in a relatively short time.

Formula for total investment

We obtained above the following formulae for investment in fixed capital, F, and for investment in inventories, J:

$$F_{t+\theta} = \frac{a}{1+c}S_t + b'\frac{\Delta P_t}{\Delta t} + d' \qquad (17)$$

$$J_{t+\theta} = e\frac{\Delta O_t}{\Delta t} \qquad (18)$$

Adding these two equations we obtain a formula for total investment, I:

$$I_{t+\theta} = \frac{a}{1+c} S_t + b' \frac{\Delta P_t}{\Delta t} + e \frac{\Delta O_t}{\Delta t} + d' \qquad (19)$$

S_t on the right-hand side depends on the *level* of economic activity at time t, while $\dfrac{\Delta P_t}{\Delta t}$ and $\dfrac{\Delta O_t}{\Delta t}$ depend on the *rate of change* in this level. The total investment thus depends, according to our theory, on both the level of economic activity and the rate of change in this level at some earlier time.

10

Statistical Illustration

The problem of time lag

We shall now apply the investment equation to the United States data for the period 1929–1940. A major problem at this point is the selection of the time lag θ.

It seems unreasonable to assume either for investment in fixed capital or investment in inventories that this time lag should be longer than one year or shorter than half a year. A longer time lag for investment in fixed capital might perhaps be assumed by some. It should be noticed, however, that United States statistics of investment in fixed capital depend on shipments of equipment and on 'value put in place' for construction. In the latter case, where the work on various structures is differently advanced, the time lag is about one half of that between starts and completions. This, of course, reduces considerably the chance that the time lag applicable to the analysis of the United States data should be more than one year. (Construction accounts for around 50 per cent of investment in fixed capital.) On the other hand, it is difficult to imagine this lag to be less than half a year especially if we take into consideration that θ also includes the delayed reaction of entrepreneurs to factors determining investment decisions. The same seems to be true of inventories. In the light of what is known about their movement, it is difficult to assume a time lag shorter than half a year. On the other hand, a time lag longer than one year seems definitely unreasonable in this case.

Having fixed the limits for the time lag, θ, we are still left with the problem of choosing the 'right' θ within these limits. This, however, appears to be an impossible task. In the case of investment in fixed capital we obtain with a one-year time lag a reasonable double correlation of investment with savings and the rate of change in profits. With a half-year time lag we obtain a close correlation of investment with savings, but the rate of change in profits has no apparent influence. (The single correlation coefficient is much higher here than the double correlation coefficient in the case of the one-year time lag.) This relation, however, in spite of the perfect fit, does not seem to be very reasonable. Apart from the fact that according to the above theory the rate of change in profits should exert at least some influence, it does not seem plausible that such a complex phenomenon as investment in fixed capital should be determined so perfectly by one variable only.[1]

The correlation between investment in inventories and the rate of change in the aggregate output appears to be much higher for a one-year than for a half-year time lag. It will be seen, however, that the low correlation coefficient in the case of a half-year time lag is largely due to the fact that investment in inventories in 1930 is considerably above the regression line. As this was the first depression year this may be interpreted as an unusually long delay in adjustment of inventories immediately after the turning point in output (see p. 107). It is thus again hard to say whether a half-year time lag is less appropriate than a one-year time lag even though the correlation coefficient in the former case is much lower.

The above discussion indicates that the 'goodness of fit' is here not an adequate criterion for the selection of the time lag. In the circumstances the only solution seems to be to produce two variants of the investment equation basing one on a one-year and the other on a half-year time lag.

Investment in fixed capital

We shall first examine the two variants for investment in fixed capital. We thus apply the equation

$$F_t = \frac{a}{1 + c} S_{t-\theta} + b' \frac{\Delta P_{t-\theta}}{\Delta t} + d' \qquad (17)$$

[1] The danger of applying the criterion of 'goodness of fit' to the determination of the time lag between investment decisions and actual investment may be illustrated by an extreme case. Imagine that foreign trade and the budget are balanced and that the volume of inventories is stable for a number of years. Then, savings are equal to investment in fixed capital for all this period. Thus, the 'best fit' for equation (17) would be obtained for $\theta = 0$. The 'regression equation' would then be $F_t = S_t$ with $\frac{a}{1 + c} = 1$, $b' = 0$, and $d' = 0$. The 'correlation coefficient' would, of course, be equal to 1.

firstly, on the assumption that $\theta = 1$, and, secondly, on the assumption that $\theta = \frac{1}{2}$.

In Table 20 the relevant data are shown for the variant $\theta = 1$. (The period covered is 1930–1940 because savings, S, and profits, P, are for the preceding year and thus the year 1929 is 'lost.')

Table 20. **Determination of Investment in Fixed Capital in the United States, 1930–1940**

Assuming $\theta = 1$

Year	Investment in fixed capital	Gross savings	Rate of change of gross profits after taxes	Calculated investment in fixed capital
	F_t	S_{t-1}	$P_{t-\frac{1}{2}} - P_{t-\frac{3}{2}}$	
	(Billions of dollars at 1939 prices)*			
1930	10·2	14·6	− 2·1	10·4
1931	7·1	10·9	− 6·6	6·7
1932	4·0	8·9	− 6·3	5·6
1933	3·5	3·3	− 5·4	2·3
1934	4·4	3·3	2·6	4·6
1935	5·8	6·2	2·9	6·5
1936	7·9	8·8	3·5	8·4
1937	9·3	12·0	2·0	10·0
1938	7·2	11·0	− 1·7	8·2
1939	9·5	8·8	− 0·7	7·1
1940	11·4	12·7	2·3	10·5

* Deflated by price index of investment goods.

Source: Department of Commerce, National Income Supplement to the Survey of Current Business, 1951. *For details see Statistical Appendix, Notes 10, 11, 12, and 13.*

Both the value of investment in fixed capital, F_t, and the value of total gross savings for the previous year, S_{t-1}, are deflated by the price index of investment goods.[1] The greatest difficulty was confronted in determining the series $\frac{\Delta P}{\Delta t}$. This was done in the following way. We estimated the value of gross

---

[1] We do not include brokerage fees in gross savings here as we did on p. 56. For although, as indicated there, it is a type of capital expenditure it does not increase the total assets of the capitalists and thus does not create entrepreneurial capital available for reinvestment. For this reason S in Table 20 is not equal to I' in Table 13. Another reason for this discrepancy is that S is deflated here by prices of investment goods while I' in Table 13 is deflated by the index implicit in the deflation of the gross income of the private sector.

111

profits after tax deflated by the price index of investment goods for the years 1928/1929, 1929/1930, 1930/1931, etc., running from mid-year to mid-year.[1] The rate of increase in profits in 1929 was calculated as the difference between profits in 1929/1930 and 1928/1929, etc. Or, in other words, the rate of change in profits in the preceding year, $\dfrac{\Delta P_{t-1}}{\Delta t}$, was calculated as $P_{t-\frac{1}{2}} - P_{t-\frac{3}{2}}$.

The correlation of investment in fixed capital, F_t, with savings of the preceding year, S_{t-1}, and the rate of increase in profits also of the preceding year, $P_{t-\frac{1}{2}} - P_{t-\frac{3}{2}}$, can now be readily established. The regression equation is as follows:

$$F_t = 0{\cdot}634 S_{t-1} + 0{\cdot}293(P_{t-\frac{1}{2}} - P_{t-\frac{3}{2}}) + 1{\cdot}76$$

The double correlation coefficient is equal to $0{\cdot}904$. The partial correlation coefficient between F_t and S_{t-1} is $0{\cdot}888$ and that between F_t and $P_{t-\frac{1}{2}} - P_{t-\frac{3}{2}}$ is $0{\cdot}684$. Investment F_t calculated from this equation is given in the last column of Table 20 for comparison with actual F_t.[2] The coefficient of S is $0{\cdot}634$ and thus conforms to our assumption that $\dfrac{a}{1+c}$ in equation (17) is less than 1 (cf. p. 105).

We shall now consider the variant $\theta = \frac{1}{2}$. As mentioned, it appears that in this case the partial correlation with change in profits may be neglected. Thus, in Table 21 there is given only F_t and $S_{t-\frac{1}{2}}$ which is calculated approximately as $\dfrac{S_{t-1} + S_t}{2}$.

The regression equation is:

$$F_t = 0{\cdot}762 S_{t-\frac{1}{2}} + 0{\cdot}29$$

The correlation coefficient is $0{\cdot}972$, which is much higher than the double correlation coefficient in the variant $\theta = 1$. The value of F_t calculated from the regression equation is given in Table 21. The coefficient $\dfrac{a}{1+c}$ is equal here to $0{\cdot}762$, which again agrees with the assumption concerning $\dfrac{a}{1+c}$ made above.

The actual F_t and the values calculated from the regression equations for both variants are plotted on scatter diagrams in

---

[1] See Statistical Appendix, Notes 12 and 13.
[2] No distinct trend appears to be involved. This is the reason why no allowance was made for trend in the correlation analysis.

112

Table 21. Determination of Investment in Fixed Capital in the
United States, 1930–1940

Assuming $\theta = \frac{1}{2}$

Year	Investment in fixed capital F_t	Gross savings $S_{t-\frac{1}{2}}$	Calculated investment in fixed capital
	(Billions of dollars at 1939 prices)		
1930	10·2	12·8	10·0
1931	7·1	9·9	7·8
1932	4·0	6·1	5·0
1933	3·5	3·3	2·8
1934	4·4	4·8	3·9
1935	5·8	7·5	6·0
1936	7·9	10·4	8·2
1937	9·3	11·5	9·1
1938	7·2	9·9	7·8
1939	9·5	10·8	8·5
1940	11·4	14·2	11·1

Source: Department of Commerce, National Income Supplement to Survey
of Current Business, 1951. *For details see Statistical Appendix, Notes*
10 *and* 11.

Fig. 9, the calculated values being taken as abscissae and the
actual values as ordinates. The regression line is a straight line
drawn at 45° through the zero point.

Some authors (for instance, Kaldor and myself) have assumed
that after investment in fixed capital has reached a certain level
in the boom it grows more slowly in response to determinants

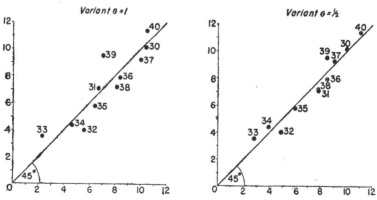

FIG. 9. Scatter diagram of calculated and actual investment in fixed capital,
United States, 1929–1940, in billions of dollars at 1939 prices. Calculated
values—abscissae, actual values—ordinates.

than in the early stage of the boom[1] and that an analogous phenomenon occurs in the slump. Our scatter diagrams do not seem to bear out this hypothesis.

Investment in inventories

We may consider first the variant $\theta = 1$. In Table 22 are shown the quantitative changes in inventories, J, and the rates of change in gross product or output of the private sector in the preceding year, $\frac{\Delta O_{t-1}}{\Delta t}$.[2] The latter is calculated (as in the case of the rate of increase in profits in Table 20) as $O_{t-\frac{1}{2}} - O_{t-\frac{3}{2}}$.

Table 22. Determination of Investment in Inventories in the United States, 1930–1940

Assuming $\theta = 1$

Year	Investment in inventories* J_t	Rate of change in gross product of the private sector $O_{t-\frac{1}{2}} - O_{t-\frac{3}{2}}$	Calculated investment in inventories
		(Billions of dollars at 1939 prices)	
1930	0	$-0\cdot9$	$-0\cdot3$
1931	$-1\cdot4$	$-8\cdot8$	$-2\cdot0$
1932	$-3\cdot0$	$-8\cdot5$	$-1\cdot9$
1933	$-1\cdot5$	$-8\cdot9$	$-2\cdot0$
1934	$0\cdot6$	$8\cdot7$	$1\cdot8$
1935	$0\cdot5$	$2\cdot6$	$0\cdot5$
1936	$2\cdot3$	$7\cdot0$	$1\cdot4$
1937	$1\cdot7$	$8\cdot6$	$1\cdot8$
1938	$-1\cdot1$	$-2\cdot2$	$-0\cdot6$
1939	$0\cdot3$	$1\cdot3$	$0\cdot2$
1940	$2\cdot1$	$7\cdot7$	$1\cdot6$

* Exclusive of farm inventories.

Source: Department of Commerce, National Income Supplement to the Survey of Current Business, 1951. *For details see Statistical Appendix, Notes 14 and 15.*

---

[1] This tendency was assumed to appear even before the stage of bottlenecks in investment goods industries was reached.

[2] Both the change in inventories, J, and the change in gross product of the private sector, O, are taken here exclusive of changes in farm inventories for the following reason. Farm inventories are affected by changes in crops which are influenced by climatic conditions not related to changes in total output of the private sector. As the weight of agriculture in total output of the private sector is much smaller than the weight of farm inventories in total inventories at the end of the year when a large part of the new harvest is still unsold, this introduces a

The regression equation of investment in inventories, J, in relation to the rate of change in output in the preceding year is as follows:

$$J_t = 0 \cdot 215(O_{t-\frac{1}{2}} - O_{t-\frac{3}{2}}) - 0 \cdot 08$$

The correlation coefficient is $0 \cdot 913$. (The presence of the constant $-0 \cdot 08$ means that inventories are changing even when output is not. In a unit of time inventories will change by $-0 \cdot 08$ in addition to the change caused by the movement of output. In other words, $-0 \cdot 08$ is a trend coefficient for inventories. It will be seen that in the period considered the trend was insignificant as compared with the changes induced by fluctuations in output.) J_t calculated from the regression equation is given in Table 22 for comparison with the actual series.

For the variant $\theta = \frac{1}{2}$ we shall correlate investment in inventories, J_t, with $O_t - O_{t-1}$. Indeed, $O_t - O_{t-1}$ gives the rate of increase in aggregate output over a period the centre of which is the end of the preceding year. Thus, the time lag between J_t and $O_t - O_{t-1}$ is half a year. The relevant data are given in Table 23.

The regression equation is

$$J_t = 0 \cdot 194(O_t - O_{t-1}) - 0 \cdot 13$$

The correlation coefficient is here only $0 \cdot 828$ and thus much lower than in the variant $\theta = 1$. (The significance of the constant member, which is here $-0 \cdot 13$, has already been discussed above.) The comparison of J_t with the value calculated from the equation (see Table 23) shows a considerable discrepancy for 1930. It is this discrepancy that is largely responsible for the relatively low correlation coefficient. As suggested above, the abnormally high level of investment in inventories in 1930 is not unnatural since it was the first year after the turning point in output.

disturbing factor. By an exclusion of changes in farm inventories both from total output and from total changes in inventories we roughly eliminate this factor. The influence of changes in agricultural output on changes in total output is considerably reduced in this way, and, in view of the small weight of agricultural output in the total output, changes in total output after the above adjustment give a good approximation of changes in non-agricultural output. This treatment corresponds to a model of an economy where cyclical fluctuations in agricultural output is of no great importance, which is reasonable from a methodological point of view.

Table 23. Determination of Changes in Inventories* in the United States, 1930–1940

Assuming $\theta = \frac{1}{2}$

Year	Investment in inventories* J_t	Rate of change in gross product of the private sector $O_t - O_{t-1}$	Calculated investment in inventories
		(Billions of dollars at 1939 prices)	
1930	0	− 8·0	− 1·7
1931	− 1·4	− 6·3	− 1·4
1932	− 3·0	− 10·0	− 2·1
1933	− 1·5	− 0·5	− 0·2
1934	0·6	6·5	1·1
1935	0·5	3·8	0·6
1936	2·3	10·1	1·8
1937	1·7	3·2	0·5
1938	− 1·1	− 4·2	− 0·9
1939	0·3	7·3	1·3
1940	2·1	8·3	1·5

* Exclusive of farm inventories.

Source: Department of Commerce, National Income Supplement to Survey of Current Business, 1951. For details see Statistical Appendix, Note 14.

Total investment

We can now obtain an equation for total investment, I_t, when $\theta = 1$ or $\frac{1}{2}$, by adding the respective regression equations for investment in fixed capital and investment in inventories. We obtain for $\theta = 1$:

$$I_t = 0\cdot634 S_{t-1} + 0\cdot293(P_{t-\frac{1}{2}} - P_{t-\frac{3}{2}})$$
$$+ 0\cdot215(O_{t-\frac{1}{2}} - O_{t-\frac{3}{2}}) + 1\cdot68$$

and for $\theta = \frac{1}{2}$:

$$I_t = 0\cdot762 S_{t-\frac{1}{2}} + 0\cdot194(O_t - O_{t-1}) + 0\cdot16$$

According to these equations, total investment is determined by both the level of economic activity and the rate of change in this level at some earlier time.

Part 5

The Business Cycle

11

The Mechanism of the Business Cycle

Equations determining the dynamic process

We shall assume in this chapter that both foreign trade and the government budget are balanced and that workers do not save. It was shown above in Chapter 5 that given this assumption the level of economic activity is determined by investment. Moreover, it was shown in Chapter 9 that investment is determined, with a certain time lag, by the level of economic activity and the rate of change in this level. It follows that investment at a given time is determined by the level and rate of change in the level of investment at some earlier time. It will be seen below that this provides the basis for an analysis of the dynamic economic process and in particular enables us to show that this process involves cyclical fluctuations.

In addition to assuming a balanced foreign trade and budget we shall also assume that the price index for deflating investment is identical with that for deflating the gross product of the private sector. This assumption is not extravagant in view of the rather small cyclical fluctuations in the ratio of prices of investment and consumption goods (see p. 27). At the same time a considerable simplification is achieved by it. Indeed, it appeared necessary above to use different deflators in different contexts for the same items. Thus, investment, savings and profits were deflated in Chapters 4 and 5 by the same price index as that used to deflate the gross product of the private sector. But in Chapter 9 investment in fixed capital, savings and profits were all deflated by the index of prices of investment goods. However, now that the deflators have been assumed identical, 'real' investment, savings and profits have one meaning only.

Let us now consider the equations which are relevant to our inquiry into the business cycle. From the assumption of a balanced foreign trade and budget it follows that saving is equal to investment:

$$S = I$$

Employing the same assumption, we may take from Chapter 4 (see p. 54) the equation relating profits after tax, P, with some time lag, to investment:

$$P_t = \frac{I_{t-\omega} + A}{1 - q} \tag{8'}$$

This equation is based: (a) on the equality between profits and investment plus capitalists' consumption; and (b) on the relation between capitalists' consumption and profits at some earlier time. (A is the stable part of capitalists' consumption and q is the coefficient of consumption out of an increment of profits.)

Furthermore, we derive from equations (10) and (9'') in Chapter 5 (see p. 67) the relation between gross product, O, and profits after tax, P:

$$O_t = \frac{P_t + B'}{1 - \alpha'} + E \tag{10'}$$

This equation reflects: (a) the factors determining the distribution of national income; (b) the system of profit taxes; and (c) the level of indirect taxes. (The constant B' and the coefficient α' reflect the 'distribution of income factors' and the system of profit taxes; the constant E stands for aggregate indirect taxes.)

Finally, Chapter 9 gives us the equation determining investment:

$$I_{t+\theta} = \frac{a}{1 + c} S_t + b' \frac{\Delta P_t}{\Delta t} + e \frac{\Delta O_t}{\Delta t} + d' \tag{19}$$

This equation expresses: (a) the relation, with a time lag, between investment in fixed capital on the one hand and savings, the rate of change in profits and the rate of change in the stock of capital equipment on the other (the effect of the change in the stock of capital being reflected in the denominator of the coefficient $\frac{a}{1 + c}$); and (b) the relation between investment in inventories and the rate of change in output.

From the latter equation and the assumed equality between savings and investment it follows:

$$I_{t+\theta} = \frac{a}{1+c}I_t + b'\frac{\Delta P_t}{\Delta t} + e\frac{\Delta O_t}{\Delta t} + d' \qquad (20)$$

The equation of the business cycle

Equations (8'), (10') and (20) apply to the dynamic process in general. At the present stage, however, we intend to concentrate on the process of the business cycle as distinct from the process of long-run development. For this purpose we shall consider a system which is *not* subject to long-run development, i.e. a system which is static except for cyclical fluctuations. It will be shown in Chapter 14 that the actual dynamic process can be analysed into (*a*) cyclical fluctuations, the pattern of which is the same as that in the static system described below; and (*b*) a smooth long-run trend.

To render our system 'static' we shall postulate that the parameters A, B' and E, which we have assumed throughout to be subject to long-run changes, are strictly constant. It follows directly then from equation (8') that:

$$\frac{\Delta P_t}{\Delta t} = \frac{1}{1-q}\frac{\Delta I_{t-\omega}}{\Delta t}$$

and from equation (10') that:

$$\frac{\Delta O_t}{\Delta t} = \frac{1}{1-\alpha'}\frac{\Delta P_t}{\Delta t}$$

or:

$$\frac{\Delta O_t}{\Delta t} = \frac{1}{(1-q)(1-\alpha')}\frac{\Delta I_{t-\omega}}{\Delta t}$$

Both the rate of change in profits and the rate of change in output are here expressed in terms of the rate of change in investment (with a certain time lag). Substituting these expressions of $\frac{\Delta P}{\Delta t}$ and $\frac{\Delta O}{\Delta t}$ in equation (20) we obtain:

$$I_{t+\theta} = \frac{a}{1+c}I_t + \frac{b'}{1-q}\frac{\Delta I_{t-\omega}}{\Delta t} + \frac{e}{(1-q)(1-\alpha')}\frac{\Delta I_{t-\omega}}{\Delta t} + d'$$

$$\text{or:}\quad I_{t+\theta} = \frac{a}{1+c}I_t + \frac{1}{1-q}\left(b' + \frac{e}{1-\alpha'}\right)\frac{\Delta I_{t-\omega}}{\Delta t} + d' \qquad (21)$$

121

Thus, investment at time $t + \theta$ is a function of investment at time t and of the rate of change in investment at time $t - \omega$. The first term on the right-hand side of the equation represents the influence on investment decisions of current savings (coefficient a) and also the negative effect of the increase in capital equipment $\left(\text{coefficient } \dfrac{1}{1 + c}\right)$. It should be remembered that $\dfrac{a}{1 + c} < 1$. The second term represents the influence of the rate of change in profits $\left(\text{coefficient } \dfrac{b'}{1 - q}\right)$ and in output $\left[\text{coefficient } \dfrac{e}{(1 - q)(1 - \alpha')}\right]$.

In line with our tentative abstraction from long-run changes we assumed above that A, B' and E are strictly constant. The same must be assumed about d', but it will be seen that in addition the level of d' must conform to another condition if the system is to be 'static.' Indeed, such a system must be capable of being at rest at the level of investment equal to depreciation, δ. For this state of the system investment, I, is permanently stable at the level δ and $\dfrac{\Delta I}{\Delta t}$ is, of course, equal to zero. Equation (21) is thus reduced to:

$$\delta = \frac{a}{1 + c}\delta + d' \tag{22}$$

which is the condition d' must fulfil if the system is to be static in the sense that there is no long-run change. By subtracting equation (22) from equation (21) we obtain:

$$I_{t+\theta} - \delta = \frac{a}{1 + c}(I_t - \delta) + \frac{1}{1 - q}\left(b' + \frac{e}{1 - \alpha'}\right)\frac{\Delta I_{t-\omega}}{\Delta t}$$

Let i denote $I - \delta$, the deviation of investment from depreciation. As δ is a constant[1] $\dfrac{\Delta i}{\Delta t} = \dfrac{\Delta I}{\Delta t}$ and we have:

$$i_{t+\theta} = \frac{a}{1 + c}i_t + \frac{1}{1 - q}\left(b' + \frac{e}{1 - \alpha'}\right)\frac{\Delta i_{t-\omega}}{\Delta t} \tag{23}$$

[1] As a matter of fact depreciation fluctuates slightly in the course of the cycle, but δ may be conceived of as the average level of depreciation.

122

This is the equation which will serve as the basis of our analysis of the mechanism of the business cycle. For the sake of convenience we shall denote:

$$\frac{1}{1-q}\left(b' + \frac{e}{1-\alpha'}\right)$$

by μ. Equation (23) can then be written as:

$$i_{t+\theta} = \frac{a}{1+c}i_t + \mu\frac{\Delta i_{t-\omega}}{\Delta t} \qquad (23')$$

The automatic business cycle

We shall now discuss the cyclical tendency inherent in equation (23'). In all of this discussion the assumption that the coefficient $\frac{a}{1+c}$ falls short of 1 is of crucial importance.

Let us imagine that we start from the position where $i_t = 0$, that is from the point A where investment is equal to depreciation (see Fig. 10). Let us imagine further that $\frac{\Delta i_{t-\omega}}{\Delta t} > 0$. This means that before A was reached investment was below but was increasing towards the level of depreciation. Now it is clear

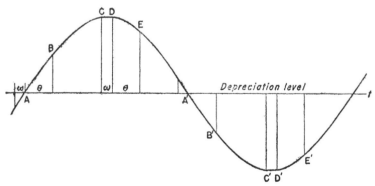

FIG. 10. Hypothetical time curve of investment.

that $i_{t+\theta}$ is positive because the first component on the right-hand side of equation (23') $\frac{a}{1+c}i_t = 0$ and the second

123

$\mu \dfrac{\Delta i_{t-\omega}}{\Delta t} > 0$. In other words, i has thus increased to point B above the depreciation level.

However, after i has become positive the question of its continuing rise, that is whether $i_{t+\theta}$ is higher than i_t, depends on the value of the coefficients $\dfrac{a}{1+c}$ and μ. Indeed, the first component of $i_{t+\theta}$, that is, $\dfrac{a}{1+c} i_t$, is lower than i_t because we assumed that the coefficient $\dfrac{a}{1+c}$ was less than 1; and this tends to reduce $i_{t+\theta}$ below the level of i_t. On the other hand, the second component $\mu \dfrac{\Delta i_{t-\omega}}{\Delta t}$ is positive because i was rising before it reached the level of i_t and this tends to increase $i_{t+\theta}$ above the level of i_t. There are, therefore, two alternatives here: that the coefficients $\dfrac{a}{1+c}$ and μ are such that the rise of investment comes finally to a halt at a point C; or that the rise continues until economic activity reaches a level where a further rise is prevented by scarcities in existing productive capacities or in available labour.

Let us consider the first alternative. After investment has come to a halt at C it cannot be maintained at this level, but must decline from D to E. Indeed, denoting the top level of i by i_{top} we have for point D:

$$i_t = i_{top}; \quad \dfrac{\Delta i_{t-\omega}}{\Delta t} = 0$$

Thus for $i_{t+\theta}$ at point E the component $\mu \dfrac{\Delta i_{t-\omega}}{\Delta t}$ is equal to zero and the component $\dfrac{a}{1+c} i_{top}$ is less than i_{top} because $\dfrac{a}{1+c} < 1$. Consequently, $i_{t+\theta}$ is less than i_{top} and investment declines from its highest level to that of point E.

Subsequently investment will move downwards, that is, $i_{t+\theta}$ will be lower than i_t for two reasons: the component $\dfrac{a}{1+c} i_t$ will be less than i_t and the component $\mu \dfrac{\Delta i_{t-\omega}}{\Delta t}$ will be negative.

124

In this way i will finally fall to zero, i.e. investment will decline to the level of depreciation.

From this point on, the pattern of the boom will be repeated in reverse in the slump. After the depreciation level has been crossed downwards at A' the decline of investment will continue until it finally comes to a halt at C'. However, investment will not be maintained in this position but will increase from D' to E' and will again reach the depreciation level.

These fluctuations in investment will be accompanied by fluctuations in incomes, output and employment. The nature of the relationship between investment on the one hand and the aggregate real income and output of the private sector on the other are set forth in Chapter 5. (Cf. also pp. 129–31 of the present chapter.)

The above mechanism of the business cycle is based on two elements. (a) When investment reaches the depreciation level from below (at point A) it does not stop at this level but crosses it, moving upwards. This happens because the rise in investment and consequently the rise in profits and in aggregate output before the depreciation level is reached causes investment to be higher than that level in the subsequent period. Static equilibrium can come into existence only if investment is at the depreciation level and if in addition it has not changed its level in the recent past. The second condition is not fulfilled at A and this is the reason why the upward movement continues. When investment reaches the depreciation level from above (at A') the situation is analogous, i.e. investment does not stop but crosses the depreciation level moving downwards.

(b) When the upward movement of investment comes to a halt it does not stay at this level, but starts to decline. This happens because the coefficient $\dfrac{a}{1+c}$ is less than 1, which reflects the negative influence upon investment of the increasing capital equipment ($c > 0$) and possibly also the factor of incomplete reinvestment of saving (if $a < 1$). If there were a full reinvestment of saving (i.e. $a = 1$) and if the accumulation of capital equipment could be disregarded (i.e. if c were negligible) the system would be maintained at its top level. But, in fact, the accumulation of capital equipment, which with a stable level of economic activity makes for a falling rate of profit, does have a tangible adverse effect on investment (i.e. c

125

is not negligible). Moreover, the reinvestment of savings may be incomplete (i.e. $a < 1$).[1] As a result, investment declines and thus the slump is started.[2]

The position at the bottom of the slump is analogous to that at the top of the boom. While the rate of profit is falling at the top of the boom because of additions to the stock of capital equipment, it is rising at the bottom of the slump because depreciation of capital equipment is not being made good.[3]

But it may be questioned whether this situation is symmetrical with that at the top of the boom. It may indeed be claimed that the effect of capital destruction upon investment decisions during the slump is much weaker than that of capital accumulation in the boom because the equipment 'destroyed' in the slump is frequently idle in any case. As a result, slumps might be very long. This possibility is, in fact, not excluded in the static system which we consider in this chapter.[4] But it should be observed that the situation is different in an economy enjoying long-run growth. It will be shown below that in such an economy the business cycle as described above is super-imposed upon the smooth long-run trend. (See Fig. 18, p. 147.) At point D', corresponding to the bottom of the slump, the level of economic activity is actually increasing at the rate of the long-run growth, while the expansion of capital equipment falls short of this rate so that the rate of profit is increasing.

The 'ceiling' and the 'floor'

The above considerations were based on the assumption that the coefficients of $\frac{a}{1+c}$ and μ are such as to cause an automatic halt to the rise of investment in the boom and to its fall in the

---

[1] The importance of the 'incomplete reinvestment' factor for the explanation of the turning point in the boom was emphasized for the first time by the late E. Rothbarth in a lecture to the Economic Society of the London School of Economics in 1939.

[2] This analysis shows clearly that the assumption $\frac{a}{1+c} < 1$ is a necessary condition for the existence of the business cycle (cf. p. 105).

[3] If $a < 1$ this will be an additional factor in the recovery of investment from the bottom of the slump. The condition $a < 1$ means in this context that fixed capital investment decisions fall in the slump less than savings, if we abstract from the influence of the rate of change in profits and in capital equipment.

[4] In such a case c is smaller, and thus $\frac{a}{1+c}$ is larger, in the depression than in the boom.

slump. In the alternative case the rise of investment in the boom will not come to a halt until hampered by shortages of equipment or labour. When this position is reached, unfilled orders will pile up rapidly while deliveries will lag behind requirements. This will result in stopping the rise or even in producing a fall of investment in inventories. Investment in fixed capital may be similarly affected by shortages in this sector. The period of execution of investment orders will lengthen and the rise of investment in fixed capital will have to taper off.

After the rise in the rate of investment has come to a halt and the level of economic activity has been maintained for some time at this 'ceiling,' the mechanism of the business cycle begins to operate. Investment starts falling, as in the case considered above, as a result of increases in the stock of capital equipment and possibly also because of an incomplete reinvestment of savings $\left(\text{which factors make } \dfrac{a}{1+c} < 1 \right)$. Having started in this fashion, the slump continues in the same way as the 'automatic' business cycle.

The question arises whether there is a 'floor' to the slump in the same sense that there is a 'ceiling' to the boom. Such a 'floor' certainly exists in the case of investment in fixed capital since its gross value cannot fall below zero. However, there is no analogous limit to disinvestment in inventories. Thus, when gross investment in fixed capital reaches the zero level, the slump may be slowed down but not halted since disinvestment in inventories may gather momentum. If, however, the slump does come to a halt the process of recovery is much like that described in the preceding section.

Explosive and damped fluctuations

Let us turn back to the case of the automatic business cycle. It appears that the cyclical fluctuations inherent in the equation

$$i_{t+\theta} = \frac{a}{1+c}i_t + \mu\frac{\Delta i_{t-\omega}}{\Delta t} \qquad (23')$$

may be stable, explosive, or damped (see Fig. 11) depending on the value of the coefficients, $\dfrac{a}{1+c}$ and μ, and the time-lags θ and ω. Given a certain set of these values the amplitude of fluctuations is constant. But if the coefficient μ is increased

127

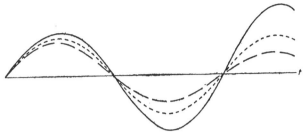

FIG. 11. Stable, damped, and explosive fluctuations.

while $\dfrac{a}{1 + c}$, θ and ω remain unchanged, the fluctuations become explosive; and if μ is reduced they become damped.

Let us first consider the case of explosive fluctuations. It is clear that, due to the increasing amplitude of the fluctuations, investment, during the boom phase, must sooner or later strike the 'ceiling.' After this, as shown above, there follows a slump, the recovery from which brings investment back again to the level of the 'ceiling,' and so on. (See Fig. 12.) The bottom of the slump is maintained at the same level because the course of the downswing is fully determined, according to equation (23′) by the level i at the top of the boom, the coefficients $\dfrac{a}{1 + c}$ and μ, and the time lags θ and ω.

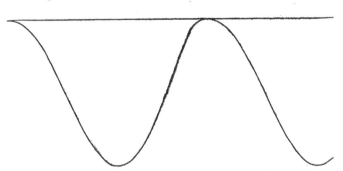

FIG. 12. Explosive fluctuations with a 'ceiling.'

In the case of damped fluctuations the amplitude will continuously decline, so that it might appear in this case that the cycle would dwindle into insignificance. This, however, is not correct, for the following reason. The relations between investment, profits and output, on which equation (23′) is based, are

128

'stochastic,' i.e. subject to random disturbances. (The deviations of the actual from the calculated values in the statistical illustrations given above may be interpreted as such disturbances.) Thus equation (23') really should be written:

$$i_{t+\theta} = \frac{a}{1+c}i_t + \mu\frac{\Delta i_{t-\omega}}{\Delta t} + \epsilon \qquad (23'')$$

where ϵ is a random disturbance. Now it appears that the effect of 'erratic shocks,' ϵ, in equation (23'') counteracts the damping inherent in the basic mechanism. As a result some sort of semi-regular cyclical movement is generated, the amplitude of which is determined by the magnitude and pattern of shocks, ϵ, and by the parameters of equation (23').[1]

This result is of considerable importance. It shows the possibility of cyclical fluctuations which do not touch the 'ceiling' and thus helps to explain the fact that such is frequently the pattern of actual fluctuations. A serious difficulty arises, however, in the application of the theory. The experiments made seem to suggest that if the damping is not weak the resulting cycle is very irregular and its amplitude is of the order of magnitude of the shocks. Since there is no reasonable basis for the assumption that the inter-relations between investment, profits and output should necessarily be such as to produce a weak damping, the value of the theory becomes questionable. This difficulty is dealt with in Chapter 13, where it is shown that if certain justifiable assumptions are made about the character of the shocks, a fairly regular cycle with a relatively large amplitude emerges even when the damping is substantial.

The business cycle and utilization of resources

It has already been stated above (see p. 125) that fluctuations in investment will cause corresponding fluctuations in economic activity as a whole. Indeed, aggregate output is related to investment through equations (8') and (10'). Also, it has been stated that aggregate output and consumption show smaller relative fluctuations than investment (see p. 63).

---

[1] It also appears that if the basic mechanism tends to produce fluctuations of a constant amplitude erratic shocks cause the cycle to become explosive. Consequently, sooner or later the 'ceiling' is reached and from then on the amplitude does not change.

We have, however, not yet examined the problem of fluctuations in the utilization of capital equipment. We shall see below that the volume of fixed capital fluctuates relatively little in the course of the cycle so that fluctuations in output reflect mainly changes in the degree of utilization of equipment.

This can be shown by the following example which is relevant to developed capitalist economies. We assume that the depreciation level is 5 per cent per annum of the average volume of fixed capital equipment and that gross investment in fixed capital fluctuates between $7 \cdot 5$ per cent and $2 \cdot 5$ per cent of this volume. Thus, investment falls in the slump to one-third of the boom level. We assume, moreover, that at the top of the boom gross investment in fixed capital constitutes 20 per cent of the aggregate output (i.e. the gross product of the private sector). Thus, since investment falls from the top of the boom to the bottom of the slump by two-thirds, the drop in investment amounts to about 13 per cent of the boom aggregate output. We further assume that the change in output, ΔO, is equal to $2 \cdot 5$ times the change in investment, ΔI.[1] It follows that the fall in output from the top of the boom to the bottom of the slump is equal to $2 \cdot 5$ times 13 per cent, that is, 33 per cent of the boom output level. Thus, output falls by about one-third from the top of the boom to the bottom of the slump. It will easily be seen that the amplitude of fluctuations is about 20 per cent of the average level.[2]

Let us now calculate the amplitude of fluctuations of the stock of capital equipment. The largest addition of fixed capital takes place in the period MN (see Fig. 13) because this is the stretch of time in which gross investment in fixed capital is over the depreciation level.

Now, the highest level of gross investment in the boom has been assumed to be $7 \cdot 5$ per cent of the average volume of the capital equipment and, therefore, with depreciation equal to 5 per cent the highest net investment is $2 \cdot 5$ per cent.[3] We assume the length of the cycle to be 10 years and thus the length of the period MN is 5 years. If throughout that period

---

[1] According to p. 67 a change in investment of ΔI in the United States in the period 1929–1940 was accompanied by a change in real income of the private sector of $2 \cdot 72 \, \Delta I$.

[2] $\frac{1}{2} \times \frac{1}{3} : (1 - \frac{1}{2} \cdot \frac{1}{3}) = \frac{1}{5}$.

[3] Maximum investment in fixed capital is approximately equal to maximum total investment; indeed, investment in inventories at the top of the boom is small because of the levelling off of the aggregate output.

investment in fixed capital were at the highest level, the total addition to the volume of capital equipment would be 12·5 per cent of its average level. In fact, however, as may be seen from Fig. 13, this addition will only be around two-thirds of 12·5 per cent or 8 per cent. Consequently, the amplitude of fluctuations

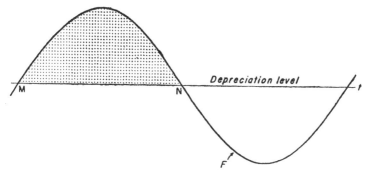

FIG. 13. The effect of fluctuations in investment in fixed capital, *F*, upon the stock of capital equipment.

in the stock of fixed capital in relation to its average level will be around 4 per cent as compared with 20 per cent for output.

It is thus clear that fluctuations in the degree of utilization of equipment are of similar order as those in aggregate output. A considerable proportion of capital equipment lies idle in the slump. Even on the average the degree of utilization throughout the business cycle will be substantially below the maximum reached during the boom. Fluctuations in the utilization of available labour parallel those in the utilization of equipment. Not only is there mass unemployment in the slump, but average employment throughout the cycle is considerably below the peak reached in the boom. The reserve of capital equipment and the reserve army of unemployed are typical features of capitalist economy at least throughout a considerable part of the cycle.

12

Statistical Illustration

Deriving the 'business cycle equation'

We shall now illustrate the above theory of the business cycle by a model based on the United States data for the period 1929-1940. This model, however, does not present an exact picture of developments in the United States in the period considered. Since it is based on equations corresponding to those underlying the theory developed in the preceding chapter, the simplifying assumptions introduced there have to be maintained. Thus, we shall continue to assume that the foreign trade and the government budget are always balanced although this was certainly not the case in the United States in the period 1929-1940. We shall also continue to assume that the price index used to deflate investment is identical with that used to deflate gross product of the private sector. Finally, we shall disregard the trend elements in the relevant equations so as to obtain pure cyclical fluctuations.

In accordance with the above we assume the equality of saving and investment:

$$S = I$$

The equation relating profits after tax, P, to investment, I, is based on that obtained on p. 58 above. Actually, the latter relates profits, P, to I', the sum of investment, export surplus, and the budget deficit.[1] However, it follows from the argument in Chapter 4 that this relation does not depend on whether I' is fully accounted for by investment, I, or whether the export surplus and budget deficit also enter the picture. Consequently, since we assume that the latter items are equal to zero, this

[1] In fact I' also includes brokerage fees.

132

relation can now be written for profits after tax, P, and investment, I.[1] We thus have (neglecting the trend element):

$$P_t = 1 \cdot 34 I_{t-\frac{1}{4}} + 13 \cdot 4$$

The relation between gross income of the private sector, Y, and profits after tax, P, may be expressed (see p. 66):

$$Y_t = 2 \cdot 03 P_t + 10 \cdot 4$$

We assume as above (see p. 67), although this again is not true of the period considered, that the difference, E, between the gross product, O, and the gross income of the private sector, Y, which is due to indirect taxes, is constant:

$$O = Y + E$$

From these equations we obtain the relation between the rate of change in profits and that in investment:

$$\frac{\Delta P_t}{\Delta t} = 1 \cdot 34 \frac{\Delta I_{t-\frac{1}{4}}}{\Delta t} \tag{24}$$

and the relation between the rate of change in gross income and that in profits and investment:

$$\frac{\Delta Y_t}{\Delta t} = 2 \cdot 03 \frac{\Delta P_t}{\Delta t} = 2 \cdot 72 \frac{\Delta I_{t-\frac{1}{4}}}{\Delta t}$$

Finally, E being a constant, the rate of change in output is equal to that in gross income and thus is related to the rate of change in investment:

$$\frac{\Delta O_t}{\Delta t} = \frac{\Delta Y_t}{\Delta t} = 2 \cdot 72 \frac{\Delta I_{t-\frac{1}{4}}}{\Delta t} \tag{25}$$

For the equation determining investment we have two variants corresponding to the assumptions of a one-year and a half-year time lag between investment and its determinants (see p. 116). For the time lag $\theta = 1$ we have

$$I_t = 0 \cdot 634 S_{t-1} + 0 \cdot 293 (P_{t-\frac{1}{2}} - P_{t-\frac{3}{2}})$$
$$+ 0 \cdot 215 (O_{t-\frac{1}{2}} - O_{t-\frac{3}{2}}) + 1 \cdot 68 \tag{26}$$

where S is savings, P profits after tax, and O aggregate output.

[1] It should be added that while we assumed in the preceding chapter, in order to simplify the presentation, that workers do not save, the present equation is to some extent affected by workers' savings. This, however, touches only the interpretation of the coefficients of equation (8′) on p. 120, but does not affect the pattern of the business cycle.

The equation corresponding to the time lag $\theta = \frac{1}{2}$ year is:

$$I_t = 0 \cdot 762S_{t-\frac{1}{2}} + 0 \cdot 194(O_t - O_{t-1}) + 0 \cdot 16 \qquad (27)$$

In obtaining the latter equations in Chapter 10, investment in fixed capital, savings, and profits were deflated by the price index of investment goods while investment and profits in the preceding equations were deflated by the price indices used to deflate gross product. Since, however, in the present model the price index of investment goods is assumed to be the same as the price index of the gross product, no problem arises on this score.

We can now substitute in the last two equations investment I for savings S. Moreover, according to equations (24) and (25) we have:

$$P_{t-\frac{1}{2}} - P_{t-\frac{3}{4}} = 1 \cdot 34(I_{t-\frac{1}{2}} - I_{t-\frac{3}{4}})$$

$$O_{t-\frac{1}{2}} - O_{t-\frac{3}{4}} = 2 \cdot 72(I_{t-\frac{1}{2}} - I_{t-\frac{3}{4}})$$

and $\qquad O_t - O_{t-1} = 2 \cdot 72(I_{t-\frac{1}{2}} - I_{t-\frac{5}{4}})$

Thus equations (26) and (27) can now be expressed in terms of investment I alone:

$$I_t = 0 \cdot 634I_{t-1} + 0 \cdot 978(I_{t-\frac{1}{2}} - I_{t-\frac{3}{4}}) + 1 \cdot 68 \qquad (28)$$

and $\qquad I_t = 0 \cdot 762I_{t-\frac{1}{2}} + 0 \cdot 528(I_{t-\frac{1}{2}} - I_{t-\frac{5}{4}}) + 0 \cdot 16 \qquad (29)$

We shall alter the first of these equations somewhat for the sake of convenience in the subsequent analysis. We introduce the approximation:

$$I_{t-\frac{1}{4}} = \tfrac{3}{4}I_t + \tfrac{1}{4}I_{t-1}$$

as a result of which equation (28) may be written:

$$I_t = 0 \cdot 634I_{t-1} + 0 \cdot 978(\tfrac{3}{4}I_{t-\frac{1}{4}} + \tfrac{1}{4}I_{t-\frac{1}{2}} - \tfrac{3}{4}I_{t-\frac{3}{4}} - \tfrac{1}{4}I_{t-\frac{1}{2}}) + 1 \cdot 68$$

or

$$I_t = 0 \cdot 634I_{t-1} + 0 \cdot 734I_{t-\frac{1}{4}} - 0 \cdot 489I_{t-\frac{3}{4}} - 0 \cdot 245I_{t-\frac{1}{2}} + 1 \cdot 68 \qquad (28')$$

Derivation of cyclical fluctuations

Let us write equations (28') and (29) obtained above, dropping the constant and substituting i, the deviation from the long-run level, for I.[1] We then have for the variant $\theta = 1$:

$$i_t = 0 \cdot 634i_{t-1} + 0 \cdot 734i_{t-\frac{1}{4}} - 0 \cdot 489i_{t-\frac{3}{4}} - 0 \cdot 245i_{t-\frac{1}{2}} \qquad (28'')$$

[1] Only if the system were actually static would i be the deviation from the depreciation level as in Chapter 10.

134

and for the variant $\theta = \frac{1}{2}$:

$$i_t = 0 \cdot 762 i_{t-\frac{1}{2}} + 0 \cdot 528 i_{t-\frac{1}{2}} - 0 \cdot 528 i_{t-\frac{3}{4}} \qquad (29')$$

Let us examine the first variant. i_t is a linear function of $i_{t-\frac{5}{8}}$, $i_{t-\frac{3}{8}}$, i_{t-1}, and $i_{t-\frac{1}{2}}$. We can add to these i_{t-2} assuming that its coefficient is zero. Thus, if we divide the time into half-yearly intervals, i is a linear function of the five preceding values of i. Let us choose as the first five values $i_0 = -2$; $i_1 = -1$; $i_2 = 0$; $i_3 = +1$ and $i_4 = +2$. From equation (28'') we can now easily determine the value of i_5. On the basis of i_1, i_2, i_3, i_4 and i_5 we can determine i_6 and so on. The results can be seen in Fig. 14. We obtain a mildly damped cycle (a damping of about $1 \cdot 5$ per

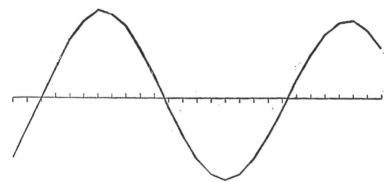

Fig. 14. Fluctuations of investment inherent in the United States 1929–1940 model, variant $\theta = 1$.

cent per annum). The period of the cycle is about 17 half-yearly intervals or $8 \cdot 5$ years.[1]

In the second variant i_t is a linear function of $i_{t-\frac{5}{8}}$, i_{t-1}, $i_{t-\frac{3}{8}}$, $i_{t-\frac{1}{2}}$ and $i_{t-\frac{1}{4}}$, the coefficients of $i_{t-\frac{1}{2}}$ and i_{t-1} being equal to zero. Thus, if we divide the time into quarterly intervals, i is a linear function of the five preceding values of i. Assuming the five initial values to be -1, $-0 \cdot 5$, 0, $+0 \cdot 5$, and $+1$, we can calculate, from equation (29') the ordinates of the time curve. This is shown in Fig. 15. We obtain a mildly explosive cycle (the increase in amplitude being about 3 per cent per annum). The period of the cycle is about 25 quarters or $6 \cdot 3$ years.[2]

[1] If the first five values of i were chosen differently this would of course affect the subsequent values of i, but finally the cycle would 'settle down' to the period and rate of change in amplitude indicated in the diagram.

[2] See preceding footnote.

135

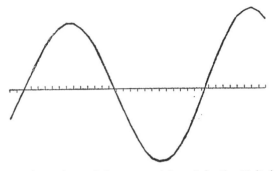

FIG. 15.   Fluctuations of investment inherent in the United States 1929–1940 model, variant $\theta = \frac{1}{2}$.

The length of major cycles is usually assumed to range from 6 to 10 years. The period of either variant lies within these limits, but the period of the first variant (8·5 years) is more typical. The cycle of this variant is slightly damped. Under the influence of shocks it would be transformed into a fairly regular cycle of constant amplitude (see Chapter 13). The cycle of the second variant is explosive. According to the above (see p. 128), it would, after some lapse of time, be transformed into a cycle of constant amplitude striking the 'ceiling.'

It may be asked how it is possible that developments in the United States in the 'thirties are represented by a damped cycle in one variant and an explosive cycle in another. It should be noticed that, as said at the beginning of this chapter, the models in question do *not* represent actual developments in the United States in the period considered because the above equations reflect only some elements of these developments being based partly on simplifying assumptions which were *not* fulfilled in actual fact. Next it should be kept in mind that the period considered covers less than two full cycles.

As already mentioned in the Foreword the statistical analysis does not aim here at obtaining the most likely coefficients of the relations considered but merely attempts to provide an illustration for the theories developed above.

13

The Business Cycle and Shocks

Illustration of the problem

It was indicated in Chapter 10 that the influence of erratic shocks prevents the damping of fluctuations in investment. That is, if a damped cycle is inherent in the equation:

$$i_t = \frac{a}{1+c}i_{t-\theta} + \mu\frac{\Delta i_{t-\theta-\omega}}{\Delta t} \qquad (23')$$

then, when ϵ_t is the erratic shock at time t, the equation:

$$i_t = \frac{a}{1+c}i_{t+\theta} + \mu\frac{\Delta i_{t-\theta-\omega}}{\Delta t} + \epsilon_t \qquad (23'')$$

will represent semi-regular undamped fluctuations. In the investigations made on the subject, it appeared, as stated above, that this cycle was fairly regular and of an amplitude appreciably greater than that of erratic shocks if the damping was mild. With heavier damping, the cycle generated became irregular and its amplitude of the same order of magnitude as that of the shocks. The above can be illustrated by the following example. The first variant of the business cycle model, obtained above from the United States data for the period 1929–1940, involves mildly damped fluctuations. The damping is about 1·5 per cent per annum and the period is 8·5 years. If we introduce erratic shocks in this model, it will be seen that fairly regular cyclical fluctuations are generated.

Our equation is:

$$i_t = 0\cdot734\,i_{t-\frac{1}{2}} + 0\cdot634\,i_{t-1} - 0\cdot489\,i_{t-\frac{3}{2}} - 0\cdot245\,i_{t-\frac{5}{2}} + \epsilon_t \qquad (28''')$$

In order to produce erratic shocks, 160 random digits ranging from 0 to 9 were excerpted from Tippetts' *Random Sampling*

137

Numbers.[1] The deviations of these digits from the mean, i.e. from 4·5, were taken to be the erratic shocks, ϵ.

The calculation of i_t from the above equation for a few unit periods is illustrated below:

t in half years	ϵ_t	i_t
0	− 2·5	− 2·5
1	+ 4·5	+ 4·5
2	+ 0·5	+ 0·5
3	− 2·5	− 2·5
4	− 0·5	− 0·5
5	− 3·5	− 5·1
6	+ 1·5	− 2·4
7	+ 2·5	− 2·3
8	− 2·5	− 2·6
9	+ 2·5	+ 0·4
10	− 1·5	− 0·5

The first five shocks, ϵ_0, ϵ_1, ϵ_2, ϵ_3, and ϵ_4, are also taken as the initial values of i_t. They thus appear both in the second and in the third column. For period 5, according to the above equation, i_0, i_1, i_2, i_3, and i_4 are multiplied by the coefficients 0·734, 0·634, −0·489, 0, and −0·245 respectively and added. This sum, plus shock ϵ_5, gives us i_5. Similarly, we multiply i_1, i_2, i_3, i_4 and i_5 by the same coefficients, and add ϵ_6 to this sum to obtain i_6, and so on. The i_t obtained correspond to half-yearly intervals. Curve A in Fig. 16 represents annual data for i, i.e. the arithmetical averages $\dfrac{i_5 + i_6}{2}$, $\dfrac{i_7 + i_8}{2}$, etc., numbered 1, 2, etc.

It will be seen that the fluctuations obtained exhibit a fairly regular cycle with an average period of about 8 years. (The period of the original damped cycle is 8·5 years.) The amplitudes of the cycles range from 12 to 25 and thus are appreciably higher than the maximum absolute magnitude of shocks, which is only 4·5.

It is clear that the mildly damped cycle of our United States model cannot claim to be the pattern of the business cycle in general. There might have been much heavier damping. Let us therefore calculate the effect of heavier damping, e.g. when

---

[1] Tippetts' tables consist of columns of figures of four digits. We took the digits of the first number, then of the second number, etc., in the first column. We used the first forty figures, thus obtaining 160 digits.

all of the coefficients except that of i_{t-1} in equation (28''') are reduced by 20 per cent. The new equation (with rounded coefficients) is thus:

$$i_t = 0 \cdot 6\, i_{t-\frac{1}{2}} + 0 \cdot 6\, i_{t-1} - 0 \cdot 4\, i_{t-\frac{3}{2}} - 0 \cdot 2\, i_{t-\frac{5}{2}} + \epsilon_t$$

The cycle based on this equation is fairly heavily damped, the damping being about 14 per cent per annum. The period is about 8 years. We now introduce in this model the same series of shocks as those employed above. The results are represented by curve B in Fig. 16. Curve B is thus the counterpart of curve A with much heavier damping.

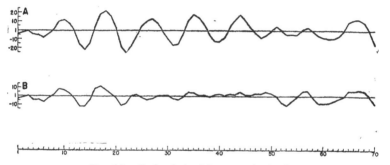

FIG. 16.   Cycles derived from erratic shocks.

The change of pattern which results from the heavier damping is easy to observe. At one stretch of the curve no regular cycle is discernible at all. The amplitude is about 12 at its highest, but is on the whole much lower, frequently sinking below the maximum absolute value of shocks (i.e. $4 \cdot 5$).

This clearly shows the difficulties involved in the above theory. It is impossible to assume that the coefficients of the 'business cycle equation' are necessarily such as to produce mild damping (as is the case in the United States model for the period 1929–1940). On the other hand, heavy damping leads to a rather irregular cycle with a small amplitude. These grounds have led some authors to venture the risky assumption that the original business cycles are not damped and that consequently they are transformed sooner or later into cycles of constant amplitude striking the 'ceiling.' However, there is no confirmation for the theory that the 'ceiling' is usually reached in the boom. We arrive, therefore, at a sort of impasse.

A solution to this problem is suggested in the next section, where I attempt to show that the difficulties encountered were due to the type of shocks considered and that another and, I think, more realistic pattern of shocks tends to generate business cycles which do not 'disintegrate' with heavier damping.

The new approach

The erratic shocks used above were of even frequency distribution, that is, the shocks with larger or smaller deviations from the mean were equally frequent. (For instance, the frequency of 5 with the deviation from the mean of $+0 \cdot 5$ was the same as that of 9 with the deviation from the mean of $+4 \cdot 5$.) In the experiments in cyclical fluctuations generated by shocks, which were first carried out by Slutsky,[1] and in specific application to economic cycles by Frisch,[2] shocks of even frequency distribution were also used.

However, random errors are usually assumed to be subject to normal frequency distribution. This is based on the hypothesis that they themselves are sums of numerous elementary errors, and on the Laplace–Liapounoff theorem according to which such sums conform to normal frequency distribution. This, in fact, constitutes the theoretical basis for the application of the least squares method.

Now, whether the erratic shocks encountered in economic phenomena can or cannot be considered sums of numerous elementary random shocks, it seems reasonable to assume that large shocks have a smaller frequency than small shocks. Thus, the assumption of normal frequency distribution appears to be more reasonable than that of even frequency distribution. An experiment which I have carried out on these lines yielded, as will be seen below, very interesting results.

In order to obtain a series of shocks of approximately normal frequency distribution, sums of fifty digits each were calculated from the Tippetts' tables referred to above.[3] The deviations of these sums from their mean (that is, from $4 \cdot 5 \times 50 = 225$)

[1] 'The Summation of Random Causes as the Source of Cyclic Processes,' *Problems of Economic Conditions*, Conjucture Institute, Moscow, 1927.
[2] *Economic Essays in Honour of Gustav Cassel*, London, 1933.
[3] Each page of these tables comprises eight columns of 50 figures of four digits. These can be read as 32 columns of 50 digits. Each of such columns was added vertically and thus 32 sums of 50 random digits each were obtained. The first four pages were handled in this way so that a series of 128 shocks with approximately normal distribution was obtained.

were subjected to the same operation as that in our first experiment. i_t was calculated first from the equation:

$$i_t = 0 \cdot 734\, i_{t-\frac{1}{2}} + 0 \cdot 634\, i_{t-1} - 0 \cdot 489\, i_{t-\frac{3}{2}} - 0 \cdot 245\, i_{t-\frac{5}{2}} + \epsilon_t \tag{28'''}$$

in which mild damping is involved; and next from the equation

$$i_t = 0 \cdot 6\, i_{t-\frac{1}{2}} + 0 \cdot 6\, i_{t-1} - 0 \cdot 4\, i_{t-\frac{3}{2}} - 0 \cdot 2\, i_{t-\frac{5}{2}} + \epsilon_t$$

in which heavier damping is inherent. The respective curves C and D are given in Fig. 17.

It will be seen immediately that the position is very different here from that in our preceding experiment. Curve D, which corresponds to much heavier damping, shows a pattern very similar to that of curve C. Both have a fairly clear-cut average period amounting for curve C to about 8 years, and for curve D to about $7 \cdot 5$ years. (The period of the original cycles is $8 \cdot 5$ and 8 years respectively.) The amplitude of curve D is only moderately smaller than that of curve C.

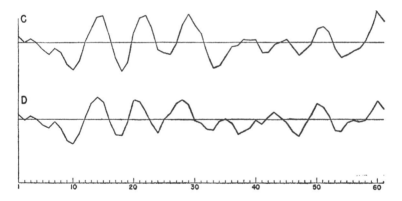

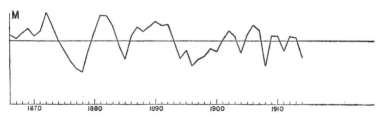

FIG. 17. Cycles derived from normally distributed erratic shocks (C and D) and actual cyclical fluctuations in the United States, 1866–1914 (M).

Although these results still require a mathematical explanation, the phenomenon itself is virtually certain: the cycle generated by shocks with a normal frequency distribution shows a considerable stability with respect to changes in the basic equation which involve substantial increases in damping. Thus, even with relatively heavy damping such shocks generate fairly regular cycles.

This result is of considerable importance. It shows that a semi-regular cycle may be in existence even though the 'business cycle equation' involves substantial damping. It thus dispenses with the necessity of accepting the explosive cycle as the general pattern of economic fluctuations which we considered unrealistic.

It may be of interest to compare the actual economic fluctuations over a number of years with the artificial series constructed above. In Fig. 17 the reader will find curve M representing the relative deviation from trend of the combined index of United States manufacturing, transport and trade for the period 1866–1914 according to Frickey.[1] The actual fluctuations differ from our shock-generated ones only in that they are somewhat less regular.

[1] E. Frickey, *Economic Fluctuations in the United States*, Cambridge, Mass., 1942.

Part 6

Long-Run Economic Development

14

The Process of Economic Development

The long-run trend and the business cycle

We have established above a number of relations between investment, profits, and aggregate output. We have emphasized at many points that certain constants in these relations are subject to long-run economic changes even though we assumed them stable for the sake of the business cycle analysis. It will be seen below that changes in these constants in the course of the long-run economic development of the capitalist economy make for the continuation of this development. This in turn causes new changes in the constants in question, and so on.

As in the analysis of the business cycle we assume here that foreign trade and the government budget are balanced and that workers do not save. Also, we continue to assume that the price indices used to deflate investment and aggregate output are identical. Thus, all of the equations used with respect to the business cycle (see p. 120) remain valid, although we shall now emphasize the long-run changes in certain constants. For this reason the constants concerned are now written with a subscript t. We thus have: (a) the equality of saving and investment,

$$S = I;$$

(b) the relation of profits to investment at some previous time,

$$P_t = \frac{I_{t-\omega} + A_t}{1 - q};$$

(c) the relation of output to profits,

$$O_t = \frac{P_t + B_t'}{1 - \alpha'} + E_t;$$

and finally, (d) the equation determining investment,

$$I_{t+\theta} = \frac{a}{1+c} S_t + b' \frac{\Delta P_t}{\Delta t} + e \frac{\Delta O_t}{\Delta t} + d_t'$$

As indicated above, A, the stable part of capitalists' consumption, B', reflecting mainly the overhead character of salaries, and E, aggregate indirect taxes, are no longer assumed to be constant as they were in the business cycle analysis, but are taken to be subject to long-run changes. Thus, they are now denoted by A_t, B_t', and E_t.

It follows from the above equations that:

$$I_{t+\theta} = \frac{a}{1+c} I_t + \frac{1}{1-q} \left(b' + \frac{e}{1-\alpha'} \right) \frac{\Delta I_{t-\omega}}{\Delta t} + L_t + d_t' \quad (30)$$

where L_t is the abbreviation for the expression:

$$\frac{1}{1-q} \left(b' + \frac{e}{1-\alpha'} \right) \frac{\Delta A_t}{\Delta t} + \frac{e}{1-\alpha'} \frac{\Delta B_t'}{\Delta t} + e \frac{\Delta E_t}{\Delta t}$$

As in the business cycle equation (p. 123) we shall denote:

$$\frac{1}{1-q} \left(b' + \frac{e}{1-\alpha'} \right)$$

by μ. Thus we have:

$$I_{t+\theta} = \frac{a}{1+c} I_t + \mu \frac{\Delta I_{t-\omega}}{\Delta t} + L_t + d_t \quad (30')$$

where $\qquad L_t = \mu \frac{\Delta A_t}{\Delta t} + \frac{e}{1-\alpha'} \frac{\Delta B_t'}{\Delta t} + e \frac{\Delta E_t}{\Delta t} \quad (31)$

$L_t + d_t'$ in equation (30') is subject to changes as a result of the long-run trend in investment, changes which in turn help to perpetuate the trend in investment. The long-run change in I will cause a long-run change in $L_t + d_t'$; this through equation (30') will effect a new long-run change in I, and so on. Let us denote the ordinate of the smooth time curve representing this long-run movement of investment by y_t. It follows from the above that y_t is a smoothly changing variable which satisfies equation (30'). Consequently:

$$y_{t+\theta} = \frac{a}{1+c} y_t + \mu \frac{\Delta y_{t-\omega}}{\Delta t} + L_t + d_t' \quad (32)$$

If we now subtract equation (32) from equation (31) and denote $I_t - y_t$ by i_t, we obtain:

$$i_{t+\theta} = \frac{a}{1+c} i_t + \mu \frac{\Delta i_{t-\theta}}{\Delta t} \qquad (23')$$

This equation is identical with the 'business cycle equation' in Chapter 10 (see p. 123). There i_t denoted the deviation of investment from the depreciation level in a static system. It was shown that, according to equation (23'), i_t fluctuates around the zero level which meant there that investment fluctuates around the depreciation level. In the present context i_t is the deviation of I_t from the trend level y_t and thus the fact that i_t satisfies equation (23') means here that investment fluctuates around the long-run trend line (see Fig. 18).

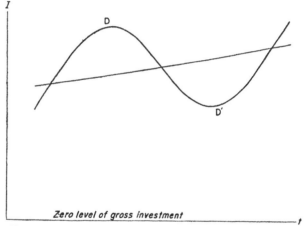

FIG. 18. Illustration of the trend and cyclical components of gross investment.

In other words we have analysed investment into its trend and cyclical components:

$$I_t = y_t + i_t$$

where y_t is subject to a smooth long-run movement related to the long-run changes in $L_t + d_t'$, and where i_t fluctuates around the zero level.

Before passing to an analysis of the process of long-run development reflected in the movement of y, it should be noticed that this process also affects the amplitude of fluctuations in i. As shown above, this amplitude is either proportionate to the magnitude of erratic shocks or is determined by the 'ceiling' of the supply of productive resources. The magnitude of shocks is clearly related to the size of the economy, the long-run growth of which tends thus to increase the magnitude of shocks. The 'ceiling' also will move more or less proportionately with the trend component y, so that the distance between the 'ceiling line' and the trend line increases with the general growth of the economy as well.

Assumption about long-run changes in L

It follows from the above that the movement of the long-run level of investment, y, is determined only if definite assumptions are made about the impact of this movement upon L and d'. We shall first consider the problem of long-run changes in L which is determined by the equation:

$$L_t = \mu \frac{\Delta A_t}{\Delta t} + \frac{e}{1 - \alpha'} \frac{\Delta B'_t}{\Delta t} + e \frac{\Delta E_t}{\Delta t} \qquad (31)$$

We shall assume as a working hypothesis that A, B' and E in the long run vary proportionately with the long-run level of investment, y; and consequently that L varies proportionately with $\frac{\Delta y}{\Delta t}$. The reasons for adopting this working hypothesis are given below.

As recalled on p. 146, A is that part of capitalists' consumption which remains stable in the short run. In the long run, however, capitalists' consumption may be assumed to show a tendency to adapt itself proportionately to the amount of profits. Thus, A may be assumed in the long run to vary proportionately with profits. It follows directly then from the equation:

$$P_t = \frac{I_{t-\omega} + A_t}{1 - q}$$

that both profits P_t and A_t in the long run vary proportionately with the long-run level of investment, $y_{t-\omega}$.[1]

As also recalled on p. 146, B' reflects the overhead character of salaries which in the short run tends to make their aggregate

[1] It will be recalled that ω is the time lag between investment and profits resulting from the time lag between profits and capitalists' consumption.

more stable than aggregate output. E represents aggregate indirect taxes which were assumed to be stable in the course of the business cycle. In the long run we can assume that B' and E vary proportionately with the aggregate output O. It then follows from the equation

$$O_t = \frac{P_t + B'_t}{1 - \alpha'} + E_t$$

that O_t, B'_t, and E vary in the long run proportionately with profits, P_t. Since profits in the long run vary, according to the above hypothesis, proportionately with the long-run level of investment, $y_{t-\omega}$, the same is true of B'_t, E_t and the aggregate output O_t. Thus we assume that A_t, B'_t, and E_t all vary proportionately in the long run with $y_{t-\omega}$, or what amounts to the same thing, that investment, profits and aggregate output vary proportionately in the long run. (This will be the case, however, only if the coefficients q and α' remain unchanged.)

It follows directly now from equation (31) that L_t varies proportionately with the *rate of change* in the long-run level of investment, $y_{t-\omega}$:

$$L_t = \sigma \frac{\Delta y_{t-\omega}}{\Delta t}$$

Our equation (32) thus becomes:

$$y_{t+\theta} = \frac{a}{1 + c} y_t + (\mu + \sigma) \frac{\Delta y_{t-\omega}}{\Delta t} + d'_t \tag{33}$$

The fact that the coefficient of $\dfrac{\Delta y_{t-\omega}}{\Delta t}$ is now not μ but $\mu + \sigma$ shows the influence of the long-run adaptation of profits and aggregate output to the long-run level of investment.

Assumption about long-run changes in d'

In order to simplify equation (33) let us denote $\dfrac{a}{1 + c}$ by n and $\mu + \sigma$ by m. We thus have:

$$y_{t+\theta} = n y_t + m \frac{\Delta y_{t-\omega}}{\Delta t} + d'_t \tag{33'}$$

Let us remember that n was postulated to be lower than 1 (see p. 105).

A special case of this equation corresponds to the 'equilibrium position' of the static system considered in Chapter 11 (see p. 122). For such a system the long-run level of investment, y, is stable and equal to depreciation, δ, so that we have:

$$y_{t+\theta} = y_t = \delta \text{ and } \frac{\Delta y_{t-\omega}}{\Delta t} = 0$$

It follows from equation (33') that:

$$\delta = n\delta + d'$$

and thus: $\qquad\qquad d' = (1 - n)\delta$

Moreover, denoting the ratio of depreciation to the stock of capital, K, by β, we have:

$$d' = (1 - n)\beta K$$

Imagine now that some factors, e.g. innovations, lift d' above the level corresponding to the static state. Imagine further that the effect of these factors is, *ceteris paribus*, the greater, the larger is the stock of capital. We thus have for the general case:

$$d'_t = (1 - n)\beta K_t + \gamma K_t$$

where γ, which is positive, measures the intensity of the 'development factors.'

We can now write equation (33') as follows:

$$y_{t+\theta} = n y_t + m\frac{\Delta y_{t-\omega}}{\Delta t} + (1 - n)\beta K_t + \gamma K_t \qquad (34)$$

The long-run trend

It is clear that the above equation is incompatible with a static system if γ is positive. Indeed, assuming that y_t is equal to depreciation, βK_t, and $\frac{\Delta y_{t-\omega}}{\Delta t} = 0$, we obtain:

$$y_{t+\theta} = \beta K_t + \gamma K_t$$

which means that investment cannot be maintained at the level of depreciation, βK_t, but tends to be higher.

Thus equation (34) represents a system in which the long-run level of investment exceeds that of depreciation. Consequently,

150

the stock of capital, K_t, increases; and so does, of course, $(1 - n)\beta K_t + \gamma K_t$, which reflects a proportionately higher depreciation, βK_t, and 'innovation effect,' γK_t. This gives a further stimulus to investment, and so on. As investment is rising the term $m\dfrac{\Delta y_{t-\omega}}{\Delta t}$ is positive which adds to the rate of increase in y_t. This latter reflects the effect of the rate of increase in profits upon investment in fixed capital and the effect of the rate of increase in aggregate output upon investment in inventories.

In other words, it is 'development factors' such as innovations which prevent the system from settling to a static position and which engender a long-run upward trend. The accumulation of capital, which results from the fact that long-run investment is above the depreciation level, increases in turn the scope of the influence of the 'development factors' and thus contributes to the maintenance of the long-run trend. The rise in profits and output which occurs as a result of the upward movement of investment makes for a higher rate of growth.

The process of adjustment

It should be noticed that the *transition* from the static state to that of the long-run upward trend is not adequately represented by equation (34). Indeed, such a transition is reflected first in a disturbance in the cyclical fluctuations; and it is through this change in the course of fluctuations that the readjustment is made. The boom is more pronounced than the slump and, as a result, a new long-run position with a higher level of investment is attained.

The change from the static state to a long-run upward trend corresponds to the change in the value of the intensity of the 'development factors,' γ, from zero to a definite positive value. Now, the same pattern applies to any change in γ or in another parameter of equation (34). A reduction in the intensity of innovations reflected in a fall in γ, for instance, will also initially cause a disturbance in the cyclical fluctuations and by means of a slump more pronounced than the boom will make for a lower long-run level of investment.

The 'trend equation' with given parameters represents in the light of the above the long-run trend to which the system has settled down *after* the process of adjustment. It will be seen below that, under certain conditions, this equation represents growth at a constant percentage rate, i.e. a uniform trend.

The uniform trend

In order to facilitate the inquiry into this problem let us first divide both sides of equation (34) by y_t:

$$\frac{y_{t+\theta}}{y_t} = n + \frac{m}{y_t}\frac{\Delta y_{t-\omega}}{\Delta t} + (1 - n)\beta\frac{K_t}{y_t} + \gamma\frac{K_t}{y_t} \qquad (34')$$

If the system *is* subject to a uniform trend at a rate of growth v, we shall have the following relations. The net investment at time t is equal to vK_t because capital grows at rate v. As depreciation is βK_t, the gross investment y_t is equal to $(\beta + v)K_t$. Thus, we have:

$$\frac{K_t}{y_t} = \frac{1}{\beta + v}$$

It follows, moreover, that gross investment y_t also increases at the rate v because it varies proportionately with the capital stock K_t. Thus:

$$\frac{1}{y_t}\frac{\Delta y_t}{\Delta t} = v$$

If we assume the rate of growth to be small (a few per cent) we obtain by neglecting the smalls of the second degree:

$$\frac{1}{y_t}\frac{\Delta y_{t-\omega}}{\Delta t} = v$$

Finally we have: $\qquad \dfrac{y_{t+\theta}}{y_t} = 1 + \theta v$

the relative growth in the period θ being θv.[1]

We thus can write equation (34'), using the above relations, as follows:

$$1 + \theta v = n + mv + \frac{(1 - n)\beta + \gamma}{\beta + v}$$

or $\qquad 1 + \dfrac{\theta - m}{1 - n}v = \dfrac{\beta + \dfrac{\gamma}{1 - n}}{\beta + v} \qquad (35)$

[1] In fact there is involved here also an approximation based on the neglection of the smalls of the second degree.

152

Since n is smaller than one, $1 - n$ is positive. The intensity of the 'development factors,' γ, is also positive.

Let us examine equation (35) graphically. We take as abscissa the rate of growth v and draw the lines corresponding to both sides of equation (35):

$$z = 1 + \frac{\theta - m}{1 - n}v \ \text{ and } \ z' = \frac{\beta + \dfrac{\gamma}{1 - n}}{\beta + v}$$

The point of intersection of these lines, if any, has as abscissa that value of v which satisfies equation (35). Thus, the existence of the point of intersection will be decisive in determining whether or not a uniform trend is possible.

z is a straight line cutting the ordinate axis at the point 0,1. (See Fig. 19, where three variants of the position of the straight line are shown.) z' is a hyperbola with the following characteristics. (a) It cuts the ordinate axis above the point 0,1 because for $v = 0$

$$z' = \frac{\beta + \dfrac{\gamma}{1 - n}}{\beta}$$

and thus $z' > 1$ since γ and $1 - n$ are positive. (b) It slopes downwards and approaches the abscissa axis assymptotically because z' falls when v is rising and approaches zero for sufficiently large values of v.

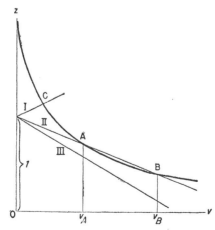

FIG. 19.   Uniform trend: determination of the rate of growth.

153

In Fig. 19 there are shown three possible positions of the straight line z obtained by varying m. In case I where $m < \theta$ the inclination of the straight line $\dfrac{\theta - m}{1 - n}$ is positive. In case II where $m > \theta$ the line slopes downward. The same is true of case III, but as $m - \theta$ is assumed to be larger than in case II the downward slope is steeper.

In case III where the straight line does not intersect the hyperbola a uniform trend clearly cannot appear because no value of the rate of growth v will satisfy equation (35). Such values of v exist, however, in cases I and II where there are one and two points of intersection respectively. We shall first consider case II.

In case II the straight line intersects the hyperbola at points A and B. The abscissae of both points satisfy equation (35). There is, however, a considerable difference in the significance of the rates of growth v_A and v_B. Indeed, let us assume that the intensity of the 'development factors,' γ, falls somewhat. This will be reflected (see Fig. 20) in a small downward shift of the hyperbola z'.

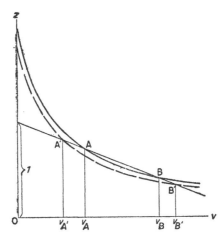

Fig. 20.   Uniform trend: analysis of stability.

It will be seen that the point of intersection A' in the new position lies to the left of point A. Thus, the rate of growth $v_{A'}$ is lower than v_A as a result of the reduction in the intensity of the 'development factors,' γ. However, the second point of

154

intersection B' lies to the *right* of the point B and thus $v_{B'}$ is *higher* than v_B. Now, it is clear that if the system were subject to the rate of growth v_B a *reduction* in the intensity of the 'development factors' could not have brought the system to a position where the rate of growth would be *higher*. In fact, there would then be a shift from position B to position A'. It will thus be seen that only the rate v_A corresponds to a stable moving equilibrium and that growth at a rate v_B is of ephemeral nature.

In case I it is easy to see that the single point of intersection, C, is of the same nature as A in case II (see Fig. 19). It can thus be concluded that in cases I and II a 'stable' uniform trend is generated (at rates of growth v_C and v_A respectively) while in case III a uniform trend cannot appear.

The three cases considered above were obtained by varying m while the other coefficients were left unchanged. Case III corresponds to the highest m. It should also be recalled that m is the coefficient of the long-run effect of the rate of change in profits and output on the level of investment. Thus, it follows that equation (34) represents a uniform trend unless the effect of the rate of change in profits and output on investment is *ceteris paribus* too strong.

Uniform and retarded growth

In the case of uniform growth both current investment and the stock of capital increase at the same constant rate. If, in addition, it is assumed as above (see p. 149) that profits and output bear in the long run a constant relationship to investment, it follows that investment, profits, output and capital all expand in the long run at the same rate. The rate of profit and the ratio of output to capital thus remain stable in the long run.

This is the familiar picture of an economy growing in *size* without a change in the *proportions* of its basic variables. Indeed, many authors assume that a uniform trend is an automatic tendency inherent in the capitalist economy. However, the process of uniform growth which emerges from our discussion is based on 'development factors,' such as innovations, in the absence of which the capitalist economy would remain static. It is for this reason that we devote the next chapter to a discussion of these factors.

At the present stage it should still be recalled that the uniform trend discussed above depends on a stable intensity of the 'development factors,' γ, i.e. on the scope of the influence of these factors increasing proportionately with the stock of capital. It is clear that if this intensity tends to decline the process of economic growth will be retarded. Capital will accumulate at a diminishing rate or, in other words, the ratio of net investment to capital will be falling. The same will be true of gross investment. From the assumption that profits and output vary in the long run proportionately with investment it follows that both the rate of profits and the ratio of output to capital will be declining. Thus, retarded growth has far-reaching repercussions upon the capitalist economy: the slowing down of the rate of progress is associated with a falling rate of profit and a reduction in the degree of utilization of capital equipment.[1]

If this process is accompanied by a shift from wages to profits, for instance, as a result of the increase in the degree of monopoly, this will not halt the decline in the rate of profit but will make the rise in under-utilization of equipment more acute (cf. p. 61). Indeed, a rise in the relative share of profits in the national income means that aggregate output will grow at a lower rate than investment and profits. Thus, output will fall even more in relation to capital than in the case of retarded growth considered above where investment, profits and output were assumed to vary proportionately although all of them were increasing at a lower rate than the stock of capital.

[1] However, if capital intensity, i.e. the ratio of real value of capital to industrial capacity, increases sufficiently, the degree of utilization may not fall. The decline in the ratio of output to capital would then merely reflect the rise in capital intensity.

15

The Development Factors

Recapitulation of the theory of investment

In order to place the factors determining the economic development of the capitalist economy in their proper perspective it is necessary to restate briefly our basic theory of investment. According to this theory, investment in fixed capital per unit of time is determined (with a time lag) by three factors: (1) by the current 'internal' gross savings of firms; (2) by the rate of increase in profits; and (3) by the rate of increase in the volume of capital equipment. The first two influences are positive and the third is negative. Investment in inventories is taken to be determined by the rate of increase in output.

Let us consider again for a moment the case of a static economy. Let us imagine that when total gross savings are equal to depreciation they accrue fully to firms and let us abstract from such 'external' factors as innovations. (Let us also continue to assume a balanced foreign trade and government budget.) It is clear that the economy can be maintained in a static state and that disturbances will bring about only cyclical fluctuations. Indeed, if gross investment in fixed capital is at the depreciation level, it will generate total gross savings which are equal to it, and as these savings accrue fully to firms they will tend to be duly reinvested. Moreover, the volume of capital equipment will be maintained at a constant level; profits and output will remain unchanged because they are determined by the level of investment; and, since output is stable, no change in inventories will occur. As long as the above conditions are fulfilled the system is static with the exception of cyclical fluctuations around the level where investment equals depreciation.

The position changes, however, if we drop some of the

157

assumptions. We shall argue that innovations tend to increase the long-run level of investment and thus make for a long-run upward trend. On the other hand the existence of current savings outside firms, which we shall call 'rentiers' savings,' tend to depress investment and thus to detract from long-run development.

Innovations

Inventions which occur in the course of a given period make certain new investment projects more attractive. The influence of this factor is analogous to that of an increase in aggregate profits which in the course of a given period makes investment projects generally more attractive than they were at the beginning of this period. Each new invention like each increase in profits gives rise to certain additional investment decisions. A steady stream of inventions in its effect upon investment is comparable to a steady rate of increase in profits. Thus such a stream adds to the level of investment per unit of time which would otherwise obtain. This is the immediate impact of new inventions upon investment. Innovations in the sense of gradual adjustments of equipment to the current state of technology are assumed to be part and parcel of 'ordinary' investment as determined by the 'normal' factors described above.

It is now clear that a steady stream of inventions adds to investment over and above the level resulting from our basic determinants. Thus, inventions transform a static system into one subject to an upward trend. It should be added that the effect of innovations upon the level of investment can be assumed *ceteris paribus* to be the higher the larger is the volume of capital equipment. In accordance with this, we assumed in our model of the trend that this effect is proportionate to the stock of capital (see p. 150). The weakening intensity of innovations is thus reflected in a decline in this effect in relation to the stock of capital. It will cause, as shown above, a retardation of the process of long-run development.

We have identified innovations here with developments in technology. However, the definition of innovations can be easily broadened to include kindred phenomena, such as, the introduction of new products which require for their manufacture new equipment, the opening up of new sources of raw materials which make necessary new investment in productive

158

and transportation facilities, etc. The above argument also applies fully to these cases.

The slowing down in the growth of capitalist economies in the later stages of their development is probably accounted for, at least partly, by the decline in the intensity of innovations. Three broad reasons may be given for such a tendency. The most obvious is the diminishing importance of opening up new sources of raw materials, etc. Another is the hampering of application of new inventions which results from the increasingly monopolistic character of capitalism. Finally, 'assembly industries,' such as those manufacturing automobiles, wireless, and other durable mass consumption goods, are gaining in importance and in such industries technological progress is largely concentrated on a 'scientific organization' of the assembly process which does not involve heavy investment.

Rentiers' savings

Let us assume that when total gross savings are equal to depreciation some outside current savings which we call 'rentiers' savings' are in existence. Thus, the 'internal' savings of firms (equal to depreciation minus rentiers' savings) are below the depreciation level which tends to depress investment below that level as well. This introduces a negative trend in the system in somewhat the same way that innovations inject a long-run upward tendency. In line with our argument in Chapter 14 rentiers' savings will tend to generate a uniform negative trend if their real value is a constant proportion of the real value of the stock of capital. If rentiers' savings are increasing in relation to capital the negative trend will be accelerated.

It is clear from the above that if the effect of innovations is combined with that of rentiers' savings it is their net effect which determines the long-run development. The trend will be positive only if innovations exert a stronger influence than rentiers' savings. It is also clear that a decline in the intensity of innovations or a rise in rentiers' savings in relation to the stock of capital will produce a retardation in this trend.

Growth in population

It is frequently assumed that growth in population is an important stimulus to economic development. It is true that if he population is stagnant, output can increase only by virtue of an increasing productivity of labour or a drawing upon the reserve army of unemployed. Thus, growing population widens the *potentialities* of the long-run expansion in output. It remains to be seen, however, whether an increase in population also provides a stimulus to long-run development which contributes to the effective use of these potentialities.

In order to answer this question let us consider a static system and superimpose on it a rising population. Since output initially remains stable, in the long run there will be an increase in unemployment. This exerts a pressure on money wages which consequently tend to fall. We are thus faced with the question whether a long-run fall in wages provides a stimulus to development in a capitalist economy.

It should be noticed first that a long-run fall in money wages—which is associated with the weakening of trade unions—will, according to our discussion in Chapter 1 (p. 18), tend to increase the degree of monopoly and thus to cause a shift from wages to profits. Far from stimulating the long-run rise in output, this, as shown above (see p. 61), will tend to affect it unfavourably.

There is, however, a channel through which the fall in money wages might, at least in theory, stimulate the long-run upward trend of a capitalist economy. A long-run fall in money wages causes a fall in prices and thus with stable output a fall in the money volume of transactions. If the supply of cash by banks is not proportionately reduced this leads in turn to a long-run fall in the short-term rate of interest and thence to a fall of the long-term rate of interest. Such a fall would be equivalent in its impact on investment to a long-run rise in profits and thus would cause an upward trend movement. But the increase in output in such a case cannot be great enough to prevent a long-run increase in unemployment; for in such a case the very cause of the trend would disappear.

It is, however, highly doubtful whether the mechanism described will be effective in increasing output at all. The connection between the fall in turnover and the fall in the short-term rate of interest is in fact fairly uncertain in the long run. If the fall in turnover continues over a long period the banking policy may easily adapt itself to this secular fall in such a way as to reduce the supply of balances *pari passu* with turnover and thus to sustain the short-term rate of interest.

It should be noticed that some authors have taken into consideration other channels through which growth in population may stimulate economic development. They have maintained that an increase in population encourages investment because the entrepreneurs can then anticipate with some certainty a broadening market for their products. What is important, however, in this context is not an increase in population but an increase in purchasing power. An increase in the number of paupers does not broaden the market. For instance, increased population does not necessarily mean a higher demand for houses; for without an increase in purchasing power the result may well be the crowding of more people into existing dwelling space.

Concluding remarks

Our analysis shows, as already stated above, that long-run development is not inherent in the capitalist economy. Thus specific 'development factors' are required to sustain a long-run upward movement. Amongst such factors we singled out innovations in the broadest sense as the most important promoter of development. Another long-run influence considered, rentiers' savings, was found to be an obstacle rather than a stimulus to development.

A decline in the intensity of innovations in the later stages of capitalist development results in a retardation of the increase in capital and output. Moreover, if the effect of the increase in the degree of monopoly upon the distribution of national income is not counteracted by other factors there will be a relative shift from wages to profits and this will constitute another reason for the slowing down of the long-run rise in output.

If the rate of expansion in output falls below the combined rate of increase in productivity of labour and in population, unemployment will show a long-run rise. According to the above this is not likely to set to work forces which would automatically mitigate the rise in unemployment by inducing a higher rate of increase in output.

Statistical Appendix

NOTES TO PART I

Note 1. Data for the period 1899–1914 are given below for:
(*a*) the value of fixed capital in U.S. manufacturing according to
Paul H. Douglas, *The Theory of Wages*; (*b*) U.S. manufacturing
production according to the National Bureau of Economic Research;
and (*c*) the value added minus wages in U.S. manufacturing according
to the Census of Manufactures.

Year	Value of fixed capital			Production	Value added minus wages in current values
	Book value	At reproduction cost	At constant prices		
1899	100	100	100	100	100
1904	137	136	138	124	130
1909	203	216	198	158	180
1914	256	280	240	186	205

Note 2. The ratio of proceeds to prime costs, the ratio of the
materials bill to the wage bill and the relative share of wages in the
value added in U.S. manufacturing discussed in Chapters 1 and 2
are based on the U.S. Census of Manufactures. The Census underwent considerable changes both in scope and method. In order to
assure reasonable comparability over the period considered (1899–
1937) the series were 'linked' in the years in which changes occurred.
1899 was chosen as the base year. Changes in the scope of the
Census took place in that year and in 1914. Since for these two years
data were available both on the 'old' and the 'new' basis, it was
possible to 'link' all the years to the base year 1899. There were also
several changes in the method of the Census: (*a*) In 1929, 1931 and
1933 the so-called work and shop supplies were included in the
value added rather than in the cost of materials as was the case in
other years. This item, according to the Census of 1904, where it is
shown separately, amounted to about 0·9 per cent of the cost of
materials. In order to allow approximately for this change, costs of
materials in 1929, 1931 and 1933 were accordingly reduced and the
value added was increased. (*b*) Prior to 1931 the tax on tobacco
manufactures was included in the value added while from 1931
onwards this item was incorporated in the cost of materials. Since
for 1931 both variants were given, it was possible to 'link' 1931
and the subsequent years to the base year 1899. (*c*) Prior to 1935
the cost of work given out was included in the value added, while
from 1935 onwards this item was included in the cost of materials.
Since for 1935 both variants were given, it was possible to link 1935
and the subsequent years to the base year 1899. The figures obtained

as a result of the above adjustments are given for selected years in the following table.

Year	Ratio of proceeds to prime costs	Ratio of materials bill to wage bill	Relative share of wages in value added
		(in percentages)	
1879	122·5	382	47·8
1889	131·7	291	44·6
1899	133·3	337	40·7
1914	131·6	370	40·2
1923	133·0	329	41·3
1929	139·4	346	36·2
1931	143·3	314	35·7
1933	142·8	331	35·0
1935	136·6	349	37·9
1937	136·3	338	38·6

Note 3. The series of the ratio of proceeds to prime costs in U.S. manufacturing, assuming stable industrial composition, was calculated by using a chain system. For instance, the ratio of proceeds to prime costs in 1889 was calculated on the assumption that the relative shares of major industrial groups in the aggregate proceeds as of 1879 obtained; this figure divided by the actual ratio of proceeds to prime costs in 1879 gave the 'link' 1889/1879. Then the 'link' 1899/1889 was similarly derived on the assumption that the relative industrial shares as of 1889 obtained and so on. The year 1899 was chosen as base in the sense that for that year the 'adjusted' ratio of proceeds to prime costs is identical with the actual ratio. The 'adjusted' series could then be built up by means of the 'links.'

The series of the ratio of the materials bill to the wage bill, assuming stable industrial composition of the materials bill, was similarly obtained. 1899 was again chosen as the base year in the above sense.

The 'adjusted' series of the relative share of wages in the value added, w', was calculated from the 'adjusted' ratio of proceeds to prime costs, k', and the 'adjusted' ratio of the materials bill to the wage bill, j', by means of the formula:

$$w' = \frac{1}{1 + (k' - 1)(j' + 1)} \tag{3'}$$

(see p. 28). As k' is calculated on the assumption of stable industrial composition of the *proceeds* and j' on the assumption of stable industrial composition of the *materials bill*, w' is the relative share of wages on the assumption of stable industrial composition of the *value added* (the latter being the difference between proceeds and the materials bill). The series k', j' and w' are given in Tables 6 and 8.

166

Note 4. The following indices for the United States during the period 1929–1941 are given below: (*a*) The index of the wage bill in manufacturing according to U.S. Department of Commerce *Survey of Current Business*, which agrees with the Census of Manufactures for the Census years. (*b*) The index of the wage and salary bill in agriculture, mining, construction, transport, and services according to U.S. Department of Commerce *National Income Supplement to Survey of Current Business*, 1951. (*c*) The combined index of these two series is taken to approximate the index of aggregate wages (see p. 37). The weights adopted are 1 : 1; the wage and salary bills of manufacturing, on the one hand, and of the industries enumerated under (*b*) on the other hand, were approximately equal in 1929, and it may be assumed that the respective wage bills also did not differ very much. (*d*) The index of the gross income of the private sector according to the *National Income Supplement*.

Year	Wage bill in manufacturing	Wage and salary bill in agriculture, mining, construction, transport and services	Combined index	Gross income of the private sector
1929	100	100	100	100
1930	80·9	90·6	85·7	86·0
1931	61·4	74·0	67·7	67·6
1932	42·3	55·0	48·6	48·3
1933	45·4	49·5	47·4	45·3
1934	58·4	55·6	57·0	54·1
1935	67·1	60·5	63·8	62·9
1936	77·7	69·6	73·6	70·1
1937	92·8	77·1	84·9	79·7

Note 5. Wages plus salaries and the gross income of the private sector in the United States in the period 1929–1941 according to the *National Income Supplement* are given on p. 168. (It is on these data that the first column in Table 12 is based.) It should be noticed that in the national balance sheet given in the *Supplement* there is a statistical discrepancy between national product derived from the income side and from the expenditure side. The figure of gross income in the second column is derived from income statistics. In order to obtain consistent data this figure is adjusted for the statistical discrepancy. (In this way we charge the statistical error fully to the income side which is justified by the fact that the data on expenditures are on the whole more reliable than those on incomes.) The adjusted gross income of the private sector is given in the third column. The adjusted wages plus salaries are assumed to be proportionate to the adjusted gross income and thus the relative share of the former in the latter is not altered by the adjustment.

167

Year	Private wages and salaries	Gross income of the private sector	Adjusted gross income of the private sector	Adjusted private wages and salaries
		(Billions of current dollars)		
1929	45·2	90·4	90·4	45·2
1930	40·7	77·8	77·1	40·4
1931	33·6	61·1	62·3	34·2
1932	25·3	43·7	45·1	26·1
1933	23·7	40·9	42·2	24·4
1934	27·4	49·0	49·8	27·9
1935	30·0	56·9	56·5	29·8
1936	33·9	68·4	64·2	34·3
1937	38·4	72·1	71·1	37·9
1938	34·6	65·0	64·9	34·5
1939	37·5	70·1	68·8	36·8
1940	41·1	79·0	77·4	40·3
1941	51·5	100·2	98·6	50·7

Note 6. The adjusted gross income of the private sector is deflated below by the index implicit in the deflation of the gross product of the private sector. (This index was obtained by dividing the current value of the gross product of the private sector by its value in constant prices as given in the *Supplement*.)

Year	Price index implicit in deflation of gross product of the private sector 1939 = 100	Adjusted gross income of the private sector	
		(Billions of current dollars)	(Billions of dollars at 1939 prices)
1929	122	90·4	74·1
1930	117	77·1	65·9
1931	105	62·3	59·3
1932	94	45·1	48·0
1933	90	42·2	46·9
1934	96	49·8	51·9
1935	98	56·5	57·7
1936	98	64·2	65·5
1937	103	71·1	69·0
1938	101	64·9	64·3
1939	100	68·8	68·8
1940	102	77·4	75·9
1941	110	98·6	89·6

NOTES TO PART II[1]

Note 7. Adjusted profits before and after taxes in current and 1939 dollars for the period 1929–1940 are given below. Adjusted profits before taxes in current dollars are obtained as the difference of the adjusted gross income of the private sector and adjusted private wages and salaries as given in Note 5. Adjusted profits after taxes are obtained by deducting *all* direct taxes both corporate and personal (direct taxes on workers having been small in the period considered). Finally, adjusted profits before and after taxes are deflated by the price index implicit in the deflation of the gross product of the private sector as given in Note 6.

Year	Adjusted profits		Adjusted profits	
	Before taxes	*After taxes*	*Before taxes*	*After taxes*
	(Billions of current dollars)		(Billions of dollars at 1939 prices)	
1929	45·2	41·2	37·0	33·7
1930	36·7	33·4	31·4	28·5
1931	28·1	25·7	26·7	24·5
1932	19·0	17·2	30·2	18·3
1933	17·8	15·8	19·8	17·6
1934	21·9	19·6	22·8	20·4
1935	26·7	23·9	27·3	24·4
1936	29·9	26·2	30·5	26·8
1937	33·2	28·8	32·2	27·9
1938	30·4	26·5	30·1	26·2
1939	32·0	28·1	32·0	28·1
1940	37·1	31·6	36·3	31·0

Note 8. The sum of gross private investment, the export surplus, the budget deficit and brokerage fees is given on p. 170. This sum is equal to gross savings plus brokerage fees (see p. 56). The corresponding 'real' values are obtained by using as a deflator the index implicit in the deflation of the gross product of the private sector (see Note 6).

Note 9. Correlating the adjusted real profits after and before tax, P and π, as given in Note 7, we obtain the following regression equation:

$$P = 0·86\pi + 0·9$$

The correlation coefficient is equal to 0·991.

---

[1] Source of data used: U.S. Department of Commerce *National Income Supplement to Survey of Current Business*, 1951.

Year	Gross private investment plus export surplus plus budget deficit plus brokerage fees	
	(Billions of current dollars)	(Billions of dollars at 1939 prices)
1929	17·3	14·2
1930	11·9	10·2
1931	5·8	5·5
1932	3·0	3·2
1933	3·1	3·4
1934	5·8	6·0
1935	8·2	8·4
1936	11·4	11·6
1937	11·1	10·8
1938	9·1	9·0
1939	12·9	12·9
1940	16·2	15·9

NOTES TO PART IV[1]

Note 10. The data on the volume of gross investment in fixed capital and the volume of the gross product of the private sector are given below. Fig. 8, which was used in the discussion of the 'acceleration principle,' is based on these data.

Year	Gross investment in fixed capital	Gross product of the private sector
	(Billions of dollars at 1939 prices)	
1929	13·5	81·5
1930	10·2	73·5
1931	7·1	67·7
1932	4·0	57·4
1933	3·5	56·5
1934	4·4	62·0
1935	5·8	67·6
1936	7·9	76·4
1937	9·3	80·9
1938	7·2	76·4
1939	9·5	83·7
1940	11·4	92·1

Correlating gross investment with gross product and with time, t, we obtain the following regression equation:

$$\text{investment} = 0\cdot306 \text{ (product} - 1\cdot45t) - 14\cdot5$$

where t is counted in years from the beginning of 1935. In Fig. 8 there are shown the deviations of both sides of this equation from the mean. Thus fluctuations in gross investment in fixed capital and fluctuations in gross product are compared after they have been reduced to the same amplitude and the intervening trend has been eliminated.

Note 11. Gross savings in current values and in 1939 prices are given below. This series differs from that in Note 8 in that brokerage fees are not included. Moreover, the 'real' value is obtained here by deflating by the price index of investment goods rather than by the price index implicit in the deflation of the gross product of the private sector. (The price index of investment goods was arrived at by dividing the current value of investment in fixed capital by its value in constant prices.)

[1] Source of data used: U.S. Department of Commerce *National Income Supplement to Survey of Current Business*, 1951.

Year	Gross savings	Price index of investment goods	Gross savings
	(Billions of current dollars)	(1939 = 100)	(Billions of dollars at 1939 prices)
1929	15·5	105·9	14·6
1930	11·2	102·9	10·9
1931	8·4	94·3	8·9
1932	2·8	85·0	3·3
1933	2·7	82·9	3·3
1934	5·6	90·9	6·2
1935	7·9	89·7	8·8
1936	11·1	92·4	12·0
1937	10·8	97·8	11·0
1938	8·9	101·4	8·8
1939	12·7	100	12·7
1940	16·0	102·6	15·6

Note 12. Profits for the years 1928/1929, 1929/1930, 1930/1931, etc., running from mid-year to mid-year are required for the statistical illustration of the theory of determination of investment in fixed capital (see p. 112). As a first approximation the averages of profits in 1928 and 1929, in 1929 and 1930, in 1930 and 1931, etc., might be taken. But this approximation is not adequate here because the series is to serve as a basis for the calculation of the rates of change in profits. It is clear that on the basis of such an approximation the rate of increase in profits in 1930 would be half of the difference between the levels in 1931 and 1929, which may obviously prove unsatisfactory. However, a second approximation can be introduced as follows. We postulate a relation between profits and private wages plus salaries which is shown here for 1929/1930 by way of example:

$$\frac{\text{Profits } 1929/1930}{\text{Wages and salaries } 1929/1930} = \frac{\frac{1}{2}(\text{Profits } 1929 + \text{Profits } 1930)}{\frac{1}{2}(\text{Wages and salaries } 1929 + \text{Wages and salaries } 1930)}$$

This hypothesis is based on the fact that the relation of profits to wages plus salaries changes rather slowly (see Table 12). It follows directly from this equation that:

$$\frac{\text{Profits } 1929/1930}{\frac{1}{2}(\text{Profits } 1929 + \text{Profits } 1930)} = \frac{\text{Wages and salaries } 1929/1930}{\frac{1}{2}(\text{Wages and salaries } 1929 + \text{Wages and salaries } 1930)}$$

Now the ratio on the right-hand side can be calculated on the basis of the *monthly* data on wages and salaries which are given in the above source. Applying this 'correction factor' to the average of profits in two successive years we obtain a second approximation for profits in the year running from the middle of the first to the middle of the second year. This calculation is shown in the table below.

Year	Adjusted profits after taxes[1]	Averages of two successive years	'Correction factor'	Profits from mid-year to mid-year
	(Billions of current dollars)			(Billions of current dollars)
1928				
				40·6[2]
1929	41·2			
		37·3	1·023	38·2
1930	33·4			
		29·5	1·003	29·6
1931	25·7			
		21·4	0·997	21·3
1932	17·2			
		16·5	0·934	15·4
1933	15·8			
		17·7	1·031	18·2
1934	19·6			
		21·7	0·989	21·5
1935	23·9			
		25·1	0·991	24·9
1936	26·2			
		27·5	1·017	27·9
1937	28·8			
		27·6	0·995	27·5
1938	26·5			
		27·3	0·992	27·1
1939	28·1			
		29·8	0·992	29·6
1940	31·6			

[1] As given in Note 7.
[2] Crudely estimated; but no significant error can be involved in view of the slowness of the changes in profits in the period concerned.

Note 13.   The profits for the years running from mid-year to mid-year obtained in the preceding note are now deflated by the price index of investment goods (see Note 11). As this index moves rather slowly averages of two successive years were deemed to be adequate as deflators for profits from mid-year to mid-year. The calculation is shown in the table on p. 174.

Note 14.   For reasons given in the footnote to p. 114 we assume in our inquiry that changes in farm inventories are excluded both from changes in total inventories and from the gross product of the private sector. This elimination is shown in the table on p. 175.

Year	Profits from mid-year to mid-year (Billions of current dollars)	Prices of investment goods (1939 = 100)	Averages of two successive years (1939 = 100)	Profits from mid-year to mid-year (Billions of dollars at 1939 prices)
1928				
	40·6		105[1]	38·7
1929		105·9		
	38·2		104·4	36·6
1930		102·9		
	29·6		98·6	30·0
1931		94·3		
	21·3		89·7	23·7
1932		85·0		
	15·4		84·0	18·3
1933		82·9		
	18·2		86·9	20·9
1934		90·9		
	21·5		90·3	23·8
1935		89·7		
	24·9		91·1	27·3
1936		92·4		
	27·9		95·1	29·3
1937		97·8		
	27·5		99·6	27·6
1938		101·4		
	27·1		100·7	26·9
1939		100		
	29·6		101·3	29·2
1940		102·6		

[1] Crudely estimated; but no significant error can be involved in view of the slowness of changes in the prices of investment goods in the period concerned.

Note 15. The gross product of the private sector for periods running from mid-year to mid-year is required for the statistical illustration of the theory of determination of investment in inventories (see p. 114). This is estimated by a method similar to that applied to profits in Note 12. The ratio of aggregate money wages and salaries to the gross product of the private sector appears to change in the period considered rather slowly (cf. the last column of the table in Note 5 with the last column of the first table on p. 175. It follows from the argument in Note 12 that we can use for the calculation of the gross product of the private sector for mid-year to mid-year periods the 'correction factors' given in that Note. The actual calculation is shown on p. 175.

Year	Investment in inventories		Gross product of the private sector	
	inclusive	exclusive	inclusive[1]	exclusive
	of investment in farm inventories			
	(Billions of dollars at 1939 prices)			
1929	1·5	1·7	81·5	81·7
1930	− 0·2	0	73·5	73·7
1931	− 1·1	− 1·4	67·7	67·4
1932	− 3·0	− 3·0	57·4	57·4
1933	− 1·8	− 1·5	56·5	56·9
1934	− 0·8	0·6	62·0	63·4
1935	0·9	0·5	67·6	67·2
1936	1·4	2·3	76·4	77·3
1937	2·1	1·7	80·9	80·5
1938	− 1·0	− 1·1	76·4	76·3
1939	0·4	0·3	83·7	83·6
1940	2·3	2·1	92·1	91·9

[1] Identical with the series given in Note 10.

Year	Gross product of the private sector[1]	Averages of two successive years	Correction factor	Gross product from mid-year to mid-year
	(Billions of dollars at 1939 prices)			(Billions of dollars at 1939 prices)
1928				80·4[2]
1929	81·7			
		77·7	1·023	79·5
1930	73·7			
		70·5	1·003	70·7
1931	67·4			
		62·4	0·997	62·2
1932	57·4			
		57·1	0·934	53·3
1933	56·9			
		60·1	1·031	62·0
1934	63·4			
		65·3	0·989	64·6
1935	67·2			
		72·3	0·991	71·6
1936	77·3			
		78·9	1·017	80·2
1937	80·5			
		78·4	0·995	78·0
1938	76·3			
		79·9	0·992	79·3
1939	83·6			
		87·7	0·992	87·0
1940	91·9			

[1] Exclusive of farm inventories as given in the preceding table.
[2] Crudely estimated; but no significant error can be involved in view of the slowness of changes in the gross product in the period concerned.

Subject Index

For Product Safety Concerns and Information please contact our EU
representative GPSR@taylorandfrancis.com Taylor & Francis Verlag GmbH,
Kaufingerstraße 24, 80331 München, Germany

Printed and bound by CPI Group (UK) Ltd, Croydon, CR0 4YY
08/05/2025
01864373-0001